# CATALOGUE OF THE HILL COLLECTION

The 'Messiah' Stradivari Violin (1716)

*Catalogue of*

# The Hill Collection
# of Musical Instruments

*in the Ashmolean Museum, Oxford*

DAVID D. BOYDEN

*London*
OXFORD UNIVERSITY PRESS
NEW YORK   TORONTO

*Oxford University Press, Ely House, London W.1*

GLASGOW NEW YORK TORONTO MELBOURNE WELLINGTON
CAPE TOWN SALISBURY IBADAN NAIROBI DAR ES SALAAM LUSAKA ADDIS ABABA
BOMBAY CALCUTTA MADRAS KARACHI LAHORE DACCA
KUALA LUMPUR SINGAPORE HONG KONG TOKYO

SBN 19 318101 0

*First published* 1969
*Reprinted* 1970

PRINTED IN GREAT BRITAIN

# FOREWORD

Although Messrs. Arthur and Alfred Hill had, in 1936, intimated to the Vice-Chancellor of the University their intention to present to Oxford a collection of outstanding musical instruments, the preparation of a gallery for its reception, no less than the political uncertainty of the period which culminated in the Second World War, delayed the opening of the Hill Music Room in the Ashmolean Museum until the year 1950.

The first and major instalment of the Hill Gift, comprising twenty instruments, as specified in the catalogue, was handed over shortly after the death of Mr. Arthur Hill in 1939 to be followed in the next year, on the death of Mr. Alfred Hill, by the violin 'Le Messie', perhaps the most notable creation of Antonio Stradivari. In 1946, a violin inlaid with black mastic by the same maker was received and, two years later, the collection of bows and the 'Alard' violin by Nicola Amati, together with one bearing the label of Antonio and Girolamo Amati.

The sole keyboard instrument included in the original gift is a virginal, in a case painted with contemporary figures in a landscape, which is signed and dated 1670 by Adam Leversidge of London.

In 1948, Mr. A. Phillips Hill, who had succeeded to the direction of the firm of W. E. Hill and Sons, presented an Italian cittern and five English guitars.

In the same year a harpsichord made in 1772 by Jacob Kirckman was received as a gift from Mrs. P. E. Bowman; and finally, in 1957 a violin by Jacob Stainer, with a date label of 1672, was bequeathed by the Reverend E. C. Tippetts.

The collection of chordophones and bows now comprises four main groups: the first and largest group, eighteen bowed instruments, illustrates viols and violins of different countries, predominantly from Italy, during three centuries. The second group contains a dozen bows, half of them English; the third, a wide variety of plucked instruments: three Italian citterns (*cetre*), five English guitars, and four true guitars; the fourth, two keyboard instruments, the one representing a somewhat simple mechanism, the other one of the most complex developments in this category.

The notion of making a collection of musical instruments first inspired the donors on the occasion of their purchasing for the third time, in 1928, 'Le Messie'. They decided then that for the sake of posterity a permanent place in some national collection must be found for so famous an instrument. For their purpose they decided eventually upon the Ashmolean Museum.

From the outset it was the intention of the donors that a catalogue of the collection should be compiled and published but neither opportunity nor anyone sufficiently qualified in the field presented themselves for many years until 1963 when, by a happy concatenation of circumstances, Professor David D. Boyden, of the University of California, who was working in Oxford on a Fulbright research grant, accepted the task of its preparation.

Neither Professor Boyden's qualifications, nor his enthusiasm, nor his scholarship could, however, have achieved publication of this catalogue had not the closest co-operation, together with a most generous subvention, been offered by Messrs. W. E. Hill and Sons, now represented by Mr. A. Phillips Hill and Mr. Desmond Hill, whose unremitting care of the instruments themselves during the past twenty-five years must here likewise be gratefully recorded. To them and to Professor David D. Boyden the gratitude of the Visitors of the Ashmolean Museum is due in no small measure.

I. G. ROBERTSON
Keeper of Western Art

20 *July* 1967

# CONTENTS

# INTRODUCTION

When Alfred and Arthur Hill assembled the instruments that became the nucleus of the present Hill Collection, it is doubtful if they were concerned as much with the systematic aspects of their collection as with the perfection, beauty, and historical interest of each instrument. As a consequence, the collection does not pretend to represent each family completely, but it is, instrument for instrument, one of the most impressive in the world, and in the field of the violin it is unsurpassed. The greatness of the Italian tradition of violin making is underscored by superb examples of the most celebrated craftsmen: the Brescian school of the sixteenth century by the work of Gasparo da Salò, and the Cremona school from the sixteenth to the eighteenth centuries by three generations of the Amati family and by Stradivari. Included are such famous instruments as a violin (1564) and a viola (1574) made by Andrea Amati for the court of Charles IX in Paris, and the 'Messiah' ('Le Messie') violin made by Antonio Stradivari in 1716. Apart from the violins, one may single out a bass viol of extraordinary shape and ornamentation (*c.* 1600) attributed to John Rose of Bridewell, a cittern by Gasparo da Salò, and a guitar by Stradivari, one of four known to exist.

The instruments and bows, contained in eight glass cases, are arranged for beauty of effect and convenience of display rather than by families. For the purposes of this catalogue, however, the instruments are described by families and within families in chronological order. On the basis of this schematic arrangement, each instrument and each bow has been assigned a permanent number which accompanies the label of the instrument or bow in the Museum and which is used in the catalogue description below.

The plates at the end of the catalogue are numbered to correspond. For example, the 'Messiah' violin of Stradivari is numbered '18', and the several plates devoted to this instrument are all labelled '18' (a, b, c, d, e, f, in this case).

The arrangement by families is as follows:

> No.  1– 7: Viol Family
> No.  8–18: Violin Family
> No. 19–30: Bows
> No. 31–33: Citterns
> No. 34–38: English Guitars
> No. 39–42: Guitars
> No. 43–44: Keyboard Instruments

The 'D.' number, furnished in connection with the descriptions of individual instruments below, refers to the number assigned to the particular instrument by Thurston Dart in his brief catalogue of the collection, printed in the *Galpin Society Journal*, vii (April, 1954), pp. 7–10.

# THE BOWED INSTRUMENTS

In this collection a majority of the instruments belongs to the category of bowed chordophones of the viol and violin families. These instruments will be described first and the plucked chordophones later.

The viol and violin families each comprise three principal members, corresponding to the treble, alto-tenor, and bass registers. In the violin family these members are called the violin, viola, and violoncello (cello), respectively. The corresponding members of the viol family, having no specific names, are known as treble viol, alto (tenor) viol, and bass viol. The Italian term 'viola da gamba' properly denotes *all* members of the viol family from the largest to the smallest, referring to their playing position 'at the leg'. In modern usage, the term 'viola da gamba' (or simply 'gamba') is often restricted to mean 'bass viol', but this limited meaning has no historical justification, dating from the time of Hector Berlioz (1803–69) when only the bass viol was remembered as a vestige of the obsolete viola da gamba family.

The origin of the viol family has never been satisfactorily investigated and is still obscure. One possibility is that the viols originated in fifteenth-century Spain as a bowed species ('vihuela de arco') of the Spanish guitar ('vihuela de mano'). However, this cannot be the whole story, and we must await a later day for a full account. In any case, by 1500 the viols had clearly emerged as fully developed instruments grouped in the three-member family described above.

The violins originated about 1520 in northern Italy as a family of three-stringed instruments, a fourth string being added about 1550. By mid-century, too, the basic form of the violin was established, and subsequent changes in construction and fitting were largely those of detail necessary to adapt the instrument to playing changes throughout the centuries.

The violins were not descended from the viols, as is sometimes claimed, and the truth of this may be deduced from the fact that the violins did not displace the viols. The latter became obsolete, not on the advent of the violins, but only when the musical conditions that nurtured the viols went out of fashion. Moreover, the violins and viols had very little in common from a constructional point of view. To the unpracticed eye, there is a certain similarity in the form of their bodies, but this similarity is more apparent than real.

The divergencies of form and construction, demonstrated by the plates at the end of this volume, may be described as follows. In the violin, the middle bouts are cut more deeply into the body of the instrument than those in the viol, and the sound holes of the violin are in the form of an 'f' while those of the viol are typically in the form of an inverted 'C'. Viols generally have sloping shoulders while the violins have rounded shoulders. (However, some bass viols have rounded shoulders similar to their counterparts, the cellos: cf. No. 7 in this catalogue.) The belly (also called 'top' or 'table') of both viols and violins is arched but with this difference: on the viols the curve of the arch is carried, as a rule, directly to the edge of the instrument, while on the violins there is usually a small depression just before the edge is reached. The edges of the violins, unlike those of the viols, project beyond the ribs. Purfling (the thin line of inlay running just inside the edge of the body) is used in both types of instruments, and even double purfling is to be found in certain viols and violins. The violin pegbox is normally surmounted by a scroll, but many viols have a carved male or female head instead of the scroll (cf. Nos. 3, 4, 5, and 6 in the present collection). Unlike violins, the viols, especially those of early date, are frequently provided with a rose hole in the upper portion of the table. In profile view, the ribs of all viols are seen to be deep, while the ribs of the violin are quite shallow. The cello, the bass of the violin family, is an exception since it has deep ribs similar to those of the viols. The back of the viol is flat and the upper half is usually inclined toward the neck, while the back of the violin is rounded through its whole length. Within the instruments, both viol and violin are reinforced by sound posts and bass bars, but the whole construction of the viol is lighter than that of the violin. The viol is made to withstand far less tension, and the wood is thinner, a fact that affects the resulting sound.

The strings of the viol are also thinner than those used on the violin and are secured at the tailpiece by a hook-bar, while the strings of the violin are attached to a tailpiece secured by a heavy loop of gut over an end-button. Normally there are six strings on the viol, requiring a broad neck and a broad fingerboard to carry them. The violin invariably has four strings (after 1550), and consequently the neck and fingerboard are narrower than those of the viol. The strings of the latter are normally tuned in fourths with a third in the middle, a typical bass-viol tuning being D G c e a d' (the treble-viol tuning is an octave higher). The violin strings are tuned entirely in fifths (g d' a' e' ') with the result that violin fingering is more uniform.

Unlike the violin, the viol has frets. The latter are pieces of gut tied firmly round the fingerboard at the position of each semitone to guide the fingers of the player. As a rule, there are seven of these frets, and, because of them, viol fingering is based essentially on a system of semitones, while violin fingering is based on the diatonic scale as a norm. Each fret acts like the nut of the violin, the result being that each stopped tone sounds more like open-string tone. Hence there is less difference in sound between the open and stopped strings of the viol than between the open and stopped strings of the violin.

There are also fundamental differences between the bowing of the two species of instruments. The viol player holds the bow underhand, while the violinist (and cellist) hold it overhand. With this overhand grip, the down-bow stroke of the violinist, influenced by the force of gravity, makes a heavier stroke than the up-bow. On the other hand, since the viol bow is held horizontally with underhand grip, there is not much difference between the weight of a bow stroke that is pushed in toward the player and one that is pulled outward, away from him. Nevertheless, since earliest times viol players have regarded 'in-bow' as a some-what more weighted stroke than 'out-bow'; and therefore in-bow on the viol is comparable in emphasis with down-bow on the violin.

All viols, from the smallest to the largest, are played and braced between the knees and legs. It was for this reason that the Italians, early in the sixteenth century, called the viols 'viole da gamba' or 'leg violas', while they called the violins, 'viole da braccio' or 'arm violas', thus distinguishing the viols from the violins by their characteristic playing positions. This terminology is not completely consistent because the cello, the bass of the violin family, was not played on the arm. How-ever, the distinction was sufficiently clear for all practical purposes throughout the sixteenth century and even into the seventeenth.

It is almost impossible to characterize a sound in words but, in the most general terms, the sound of the viols is thinner, reedier, and more transparent than that of the violin. This is so because the viols are under less tension and use thinner strings. Other contributing factors are the frets, the greater use of open strings, the manner of bowing, and, in some respects, the difference of technique (the sparse use of vibrato is an instance). On the whole, the sound of the viol is rather more impersonal than that of the violin, which is relatively assertive, penetrating, and expressive.

In any case, the violin proved more adaptable to musical needs and changes than the viol. The latter was heard at its best in the forms of polyphonic ensemble music like the fancy (fantasia), where the transparency of the sound of the viol was an advantage in attaining a clear texture of the whole ensemble. In the sixteenth century, the violin was associated mainly with dance music. In the seventeenth century, it continued to be used for this purpose but it was also eminently suited to the expressive demands of a new music, including the opera and the sonata. Indeed, in the formal development of the latter the violin played a leading part. At the same time, the traditional forms of viol music began to fall from fashion, and the viols were not particularly suited to the new styles. As a result, the violins emerged by 1700 as the dominant stringed instruments in the orchestra and as soloists in the sonata and the concerto, while the viols gradually declined through waning popularity to obsolescence. With the exception of the bass member, the viol family was virtually obsolete by the end of the seventeenth century, and shortly after 1750 the bass viol also passed from the centre of the musical stage.

These historical facts are reflected in some measure by the Hill Collection. The viols are relatively early and there is only one treble, while the violins span three centuries—the sixteenth, seventeenth, and eighteenth—all of which are represented by equally remarkable examples.

# VIOLS

Unless otherwise noted, the pegs and bridges of the viols are not original but are restored in appropriate style. All the viols have six strings and are fretted with gut.

1 (D. 4:5) TREBLE VIOL by Giovanni Maria of Brescia, Venice, probably made between 1500 and 1525.
Plate 1 (a, b, c)
Label: Juan Maria da Bressa:
fece in Venecia

The body is varnished a dark, golden-brown colour, much faded in front. A guitar form of body is used rather than one with sharply defined bouts. The table (top) is made of open-grained pine, the back in one piece of figured maple cut on the slab, the sides of similar wood, and the head of plain wood. The scroll is rather primitive in form: there are no protruding ears, and a single flute at the front of the scroll merges into a triple flute at the back. The usual C-holes are slightly decorated (cf. Pl. 1a), and a single line of purfling graces the front and back. The neck, fingerboard, pegbox, scroll, and tailpiece are all original.

This instrument is one of the oldest and best preserved treble viols extant. It is difficult to date. The maker's son, Giovanni Giacobo dalla Corna of Brescia, lived from about 1485 to about 1550. The father consequently must have been born at least twenty years earlier, so that by 1525 he must have been at least sixty years old— a fairly ripe age for the sixteenth century. Still, Giovanni Maria (the father) may have been making instruments about or even after 1525 (cf. the remarks to No. 8, below). The label is printed in a Rotunda type common about 1500–20 and not used after 1560. The tenuous evidence of the label and the form of the body suggest that this treble viol was made between 1500 and 1525.

Hill Gift, 1939.                                    *Annual Report*, 1939, p. 27[1]

| MEASUREMENTS | Inches | Millimetres |
|---|---|---|
| Length overall | 24½ | 622 |
| Length of body[2] | 14⅛ | 358 |
| Width, upper bouts | 7 | 178 |
| Width, centre bouts | 5⁷⁄₁₆ | 137 |
| Width, lower bouts | 8½ | 215 |
| Depth of sides | 2¾ | 70 |
| Length of fingerboard | 8⅜ | 213 |
| String length | 12⅜ | 314 |

# 2

(D. 2:1) BASS VIOL made by Gasparo (Bertolotti) da Salò (1540–1609), Brescia, late sixteenth century.
Plate 2 (a, b, c)
Label:                          Gaspar da Salò in Brescia [no date]

The body of this instrument is rather unusual, having rounded shoulders and highly placed middle bouts with pointed corners and highly placed C-holes, the latter of decorated form. Note, too, the ridge-cut running upward from the upper corners of the middle bouts and downward from the lower corners. The table is made of a golden-brown wood, called 'cedar of Lebanon',[3] of irregular cross grain, giving a most unusual lattice effect (cf. No. 9 and 31). There is a carved rose hole, and double

[1] The full title of these annual reports is *Report of the Visitors of the Ashmolean Museum.*
[2] Wherever measurements involve curved surfaces as here, the measurement is taken over the curve.
[3] Cedar of Lebanon was a species of tree common in the surroundings of Lake Garda. Salò, where Gasparo was born and lived his early life, is on the southwest shore of Lake Garda.

lines of purfling adorn the edges, front and back. The back, flat and tapering to the shoulders, is made of two pieces of figured maple varnished a light golden-brown. The same material is used for the ribs, which are bordered by a beaded edge. The scroll (like No. 1) has a single flute merging into a triple flute at the back. The neck and fingerboard are original, but the tailpiece, although in the same style, is probably of a later date. There is no sound post (and there never was one), the table being strengthened by a bass bar running down the middle.

Hill Gift, 1939.                                    *Annual Report*, 1939, p. 27.

| MEASUREMENTS | *Inches* | *Millimetres* |
|---|---|---|
| Length overall | $45\frac{3}{4}$ | 1163 |
| Length of body | $26\frac{3}{4}$ | 680 |
| Width, upper bouts | $13\frac{1}{4}$ | 337 |
| Width, centre bouts | $9\frac{1}{8}$ | 232 |
| Width, lower bouts | $16\frac{1}{2}$ | 420 |
| Depth of sides[1] | $4\frac{3}{8}$–$5\frac{1}{4}$ | 112–133 |
| Length of fingerboard | 17 | 432 |
| String length | $25\frac{1}{4}$ | 642 |

3 (D. 2:3) BASS VIOL, Venetian (maker unknown), sixteenth century.
Plate 3 (a, b, c, d, e, f)
Label: none

The body outline is similar to that of No. 2 (shoulder, placement of middle bouts, sharp corners, and ridge-cut), but the sound post and bass bar are in normal position. Note the inverted and decorated form of the sound holes. The rose hole is recessed.

   The top, dark brown in colour, is made of ordinary pine of coarse, wide grain. Besides the single purfling, the table is elaborately inlaid with designs of multi-coloured woods and ivory. The back is made of dark brown walnut, and is flat with a bevelling to the shoulders, more pronounced than in No. 2. There is no purfling on the back. The ribs, set into a beaded edge, are made of sycamore. The elaborately carved pegbox is capped by a male head of rather sinister expression (Pl. 3d, e, f). The pegbox and hook-bar are undoubtedly original, but the neck, fingerboard, and tailpiece are not. The bridge, while not original, appears to be old.

Hill Gift, 1939.                                    *Annual Report*, 1939, p. 27.

[1] Here and subsequently the first figure in the 'depth of sides' measurement is that taken at the top of the instrument viewed when standing up in the case. Unless otherwise noted, the second figure is that taken at the bottom of the instrument.

8

| MEASUREMENTS | Inches | Millimetres |
|---|---|---|
| Length overall | $43\frac{1}{2}$ | 1105 |
| Length of body | $23\frac{3}{4}$ | 604 |
| Width, upper bouts | $13\frac{3}{4}$ | 349 |
| Width, centre bouts | $8\frac{5}{8}$ | 219 |
| Width, lower bouts | 16 | 407 |
| Depth of sides | $4-5\frac{3}{4}$ | 102–146 |
| Length of fingerboard | $14\frac{3}{8}$ | 365 |
| String length | $24\frac{1}{8}$ | 613 |

4 (D. 7:2) BASS VIOL, attributed to John Rose of Bridewell, London, *c.* 1600. Plate 4 (a, b, c, d, e, f)
Label: none

The elaborations of the scalloped outline of this large bass viol are matched by those of the inlay on the table, back, and sides. The wood of the table, made of finely grained pine and varnished a golden colour, is decorated with floral designs done with a hot needle (*point-d'aiguille*). The sound holes, modelled on the 'flaming-sword' pattern and bordered by inlay, are themselves treated as an intrinsic part of the floral decoration. The double-purfled edges of the instrument are typically English. The centre of the table is painted with the arms of Sir Charles Somerset (*c.* 1585–1665), the head of whose family is the Duke of Beaufort—hence this instrument is sometimes called 'the Beaufort viol'. What may be a coat of arms is carved on the back of the pegbox (Pl. 4f) but it is unrelated to the painted coat of arms on the table. The back and sides are made of rosewood, varnished a rich red-brown and inlaid with five-branch purfling of tulip wood of intricate design. The instrument has the usual sound post and bass bar. The pegbox is decorated with elaborate carving and is surmounted by a handsome female head (Pl. 4e). The fingerboard, neck, pegbox, and head are all original, but the pegs are not. The lower part of the pegbox is cut away (Pl. 4d), as was frequently done at this time, so that the outside strings would not rub against the sides.

While there is no label, the attribution to John Rose is quite likely since the ornate body outline and other features are characteristic of his work. Rose (or Ross, as he is sometimes called) was one of the most famous makers in England at a time when English viol makers were without a peer in Europe. Here one sees an example of the organic relationship between music and instrument making. The English excelled in music for viols at this time, and excellent makers appeared at the same time, producing first-class viols for professional players who needed them and for wealthy amateurs who could afford them.

Of English viols, Thomas Mace says (*Musick's Monument*, 1676): 'There are no better in the world than those of Aldred, Jay, Smith, (yet the highest in esteem are) Bolles, and Ross [Rose] . . .'. Rose's reputation was so great that he was granted a lease for a workshop in what was formerly the state apartments of Henry VIII in Bridewell Hospital (London). According to the court books under date of 9 August 1561: 'Forasmuch as John Rose, now an inhabitant of Bridewell, hath, to his great cost and charges, builded and erected a small lodging within the same . . . and the said Rose hath a most valuable gift, given of God, in the making of instruments . . . and inasmuch as his name is commended both for virtue and cunning in Italy no less than in his native country, we have granted for the term of his life and that of his good wife [Joan] that they shall continue as tenants of Bridewell and possess the rooms which he now possesseth: that is to say, one great chamber sometimes called the chamber of presence . . .'[1]

According to a letter from Mr. Alfred Hill (2 January 1940), this Rose viol was purchased by the donors 'in Madrid from one of the distinguished families residing there.' The appearance of this instrument in Madrid implies *per se* an European appreciation of English makers.

The date of this 'Rose' viol is not easy to fix. An analysis of the coat of arms, painted on the table of the viol, permits us to fix the date as not before 1598 (thanks to information furnished by Michael Maclagan, Senior Tutor of Trinity College, Oxford). Sir Charles Somerset is the only member of his family who is positively cited as using this coat of arms, and since Sir Charles was only about fifteen years old in 1600, it is not likely that the viol was made much earlier. On the other hand, we cannot know exactly how much later the viol might have been made because we do not know when John Rose of Bridewell died (even if we accept the probability that Rose was indeed the maker). There is a record of the will of a John Rose being proved in 1596 but this is definitely not John Rose, the viol maker. If Rose was already established as a gifted maker in 1561 (see above), he must have been well over sixty by the year 1600. If, as we suspect, the viol was made by John Rose in his old age for the young Sir Charles Somerset, the date may well be *c*. 1600.

A bass viol with the label 'John Ross, 1609' was lent by Noel Dilks to the Galpin Society Exhibition in 1951 (No. 508), but the authenticity of this viol cannot be vouched for since it has only four strings.

Hill Gift, 1939.                                                          *Annual Report*, 1939, p. 27.

---

[1] Edward Geoffrey O'Donoghue, *Bridewell Hospital: Palace, Prison, Schools from the earliest times to the Death of Elizabeth* (London, 1923), pp. 63–64.

| MEASUREMENTS | *Inches* | *Millimetres* |
|---|---|---|
| Length overall | 51½ | 1298 |
| Length of body | 27¾ | 706 |
| Width, upper bouts | 12⅝ | 320 |
| Width, centre bouts | 10 | 255 |
| Width, lower bouts | 15¾ | 400 |
| Depth of sides | 5 | 122 |
| Length of fingerboard | 19½ | 495 |
| String length | 29⅛ | 740 |

# 5 (D. 7:3) SMALL BASS (LYRA[1]) VIOL by John Rose, London, 1598.
Plate 5 (a, b, c, d, e, f)
Label:
John Rose
1598

This is a viol of typical form, varnished a golden brown, front and back. The table of finely grained pine is not original but an excellent replacement made by W. E. Hill & Sons before 1900. The sides and back are bird's eye maple, the flat back tapering to the shoulders. Double purfling is used on front and back, and geometric inlaid designs decorate the back and ribs. C-holes are normal in pattern. While the hook-bar, pegs, neck, fingerboard, and tailpiece have all been replaced, the pegbox and head are original, the latter being in the form of a bearded male with ruby lips and golden hair (Pl. 5d, e, f). Carving adorns the side and back of the pegbox.

Like No. 4 (q.v.), this viol must have been made toward the end of Rose's career.

Hill Gift, 1939.

| MEASUREMENTS | *Inches* | *Millimetres* |
|---|---|---|
| Length overall | 41½ | 1055 |
| Length of body | 23⅛ | 587 |
| Width, upper bouts | 10 | 253 |
| Width, centre bouts | 7⅛ | 180 |
| Width, lower bouts | 12 1/16 | 323 |
| Depth of sides | 4½ | 114 |
| Length of fingerboard | 16½ | 420 |
| String length | 23¼ | 591 |

[1] The term 'lyra' in the description of No. 5 and No. 6 is used to underline the fact that a small bass viol could be used to play 'lyra-way'—that is, with variable and special tunings intended to facilitate chord playing and to increase the resonance in the key of the piece.

**6** (D. 7:1) SMALL BASS (LYRA) VIOL by Richard Blunt, London, 1605.
Plate 6 (a, b, c, d, e, f)
Label: none in the instrument at present. However, Mr. Desmond Hill says: 'my records state that it is the work of "Richard Blunt, dwelling in London in Fetter Lane, 1605". This is the wording of the manuscript label which should be inside.' According to Thurston Dart, who followed earlier indications of the Museum, the maker's name is Richard Blanke, but there seems to be no evidence for this attribution. This viol was formerly in the possession of John Constable, R.A.

The table consists of five strips of finely grained pine, covered with light golden varnish. Double purfling decorates the front and back. The body outline is similar to No. 5, the C-holes are typical, and the two-piece back and the sides consist of figured maple. The back is flat, tapering to the shoulders. The pegbox and head are original, the latter being a carved male head crowned with a wreath (Pl. 6d, e, f). The side and back of the pegbox are carved with a floral design (Pl. 6e, f), and the lower part of the pegbox is cut away (Pl. 6d) for the same reason as in No. 4 (q.v.). The pegs and probably the hook-bar are not original; and the neck, fingerboard, and tailpiece have been restored in appropriate 'old' style.

Hill Gift, 1939.

| MEASUREMENTS | Inches | Millimetres |
|---|---|---|
| Length overall | $41\frac{1}{4}$ | 1048 |
| Length of body | $22\frac{3}{4}$ | 578 |
| Width, upper bouts | $10\frac{1}{2}$ | 268 |
| Width, centre bouts | $7\frac{3}{4}$ | 192 |
| Width, lower bouts | $12\frac{5}{8}$ | 322 |
| Depth of sides | $4\frac{1}{8}$ | 105 |
| Length of fingerboard | $16\frac{1}{2}$ | 420 |
| String length | $23\frac{1}{8}$ | 587 |

**7** (D. 8:7) BASS VIOL WITH CERTAIN FEATURES OF A CELLO by Antonius & Hieronymus Amati (the 'brothers Amati'), Cremona, 1611.
Plate 7 (a, b, c)
Label:             Antonius, & Hieronymus fr. Amat(i)
                   Cremonen Andreae fil. F. 1611

In construction this instrument has the outline of a cello with typical f-holes. Furthermore, a tailpiece is used (although the end button is not fitted for a cello end-pin), not the characteristic hook-bar of the viol, and the back is rounded like a cello.

However, the body length is closer to a bass viol than to a cello, there is a vestige of the sloping shoulders of the viol (Pl. 7a), and in the profile view (Pl. 7b), the upper part of the back is levelled off and inclined in a straight line toward the neck, as is usual in a viol. The broad neck and six strings are also characteristic of the viol. But neither neck nor fingerboard are original; and while the pegbox was clearly made for six strings, one cannot be sure that this pegbox belonged to the original instrument.

The table is made of two pieces of finely grained pine. 'Wings'[1] are set on each side of the lower bouts. The back and sides are made of figured maple, varnished a golden brown like the table. The beautifully cut scroll and sound holes, follow the same pattern found in the makers' cellos. The button of the back is branded with the initial 'M' (see Pl. 7c), signifying that this instrument belonged at one time to a collection of the Medici family.[2]

The 'brothers Amati' belong to the second generation of that famous Cremona family, being the sons of Andrea Amati (see No. 10), the founder of the family and of the Cremona school. Antonio Amati (born c. 1540, death date unknown) was much older than his brother Girolamo (=Hieronymus: 1561–1630), and apparently sold out his share of the partnership to his younger brother in 1588, eight years after the death of the father.[3] If this is so, our viol-cello and a number of other instruments by the 'brothers' may well have been the work of Hieronymus (Girolamo), generally considered more gifted than his elder brother.

The cello features of this instrument reflect the fact that there was some mutual influence of the viol and violin families on each other. The cello influence on this particular instrument may well be a sign of the times in Italy. The violin family was rapidly driving out the viol family, which was nearly obsolete in Italy by 1640. However, a cello-shaped viol may be found later in England. Christopher Simpson's *Division Viol*, a treatise first published in 1659, shows two species of bass viols, one with the typical sloping shoulders of the viol, and the other with the cello-like shape similar to this Amati. Simpson comments that viols of this cello-like shape are 'better for sound' ['resonantior'] (see second ed., 1667, facing p. 1).

Hill Gift, 1939.                                     *Annual Report*, 1939, p. 27.

[1] A term for small pieces of wood inserted on the sides of the lower or upper bouts if the original piece of wood is not sufficiently wide. These small pieces are often fashioned of the wood cut from the middle bouts. 'Wings' on viols or violins should not be confused with cittern 'wings' (see p. 36, note 1, below).

[2] A tenor of the same construction by the 'brothers Amati', similarly branded with the initial 'M' (and hence quite probably made for a set of which our viol-cello was a part), is now in the collection of instruments in the Moscow Conservatory. Although the 'brothers Amati' made many violins, violas, and cellos, these two viol-cellos are the only examples of this hybrid form presently known to exist.

[3] For these dates see Carlo Bonetti, "La Genealogia degli Amati-Liutai e il Primato della Scuola Liutistica Cremonese" in *Bollettino Storico Cremonese*. Series II, Anno III (Vol. viii), Cremona, 1938.

| MEASUREMENTS | *Inches* | *Millimetres* |
|---|---|---|
| Length overall | 43¼ | 1099 |
| Length of body | 24¾ | 629 |
| Width, upper bouts | 12⅞ | 327 |
| Width, centre bouts | 8½ | 216 |
| Width, lower bouts | 15¾ | 400 |
| Depth of sides | 4 | 102 |
| Length of fingerboard | 18⅛ | 460 |
| String length | 24¼ | 616 |

# VIOLINS

All the violins and violas have four strings (there are no cellos). They also have sound posts and bass bars, but none of these is original.

**8** (D. 4:1) LIRA DA BRACCIO by Giovanni Maria of Brescia, made in Venice, *c.* 1525.
Plate 8 (a, b, c, d, e, f)
Label:                          Gioan maria bresiano
                                in Venetia [no date]

This instrument has seven strings, two of them running off the fingerboard—the so-called 'bourdons'. The body is varnished a golden-brown colour. The table is pine of irregular grain, while the ribs and one-piece back are figured maple. The top and back are arched, the purfling is single, and the sound holes of f-form are rather primitive in design. The indentation of the body at the tailpiece end is characteristic of the lira da braccio at this time. The pegbox of trefoil design with seven frontal pegs (Pl. 8d, e, f) has intricate arabesques on the front and sides. The fingerboard is flat. The pegbox, neck, and fingerboard are original, and the tailpiece probably is. The bridge, however, is not original but is restored in old style, being quite flat in arch. There is a sound post but no bass bar.

As in the case of the treble viol by Giovanni Maria (No. 1), dating is a difficult problem. It is probable that the lira da braccio should be dated somewhat later than the viol. If Giovanni Maria was at least sixty years old in 1525 (see remarks to No. 1 above), it is statistically unlikely that he lived to make instruments very much after this date. However, two points in connection with the lira da braccio suggest a date after 1520: 1) the 'moresque' style of the arabesques on the pegbox (Pl. 8d), which probably did not come in much before 1520; and 2) the form of the body, which is the late, developed form of the lira da braccio—hence the suggested date *c.* 1525.

That the label is original is doubtful. According to the Oxford expert, H. G. Carter, the label is set in Petit Canon Roman of Robert Grandjean, used not earlier than 1570. If this is correct, then either a) the instrument was made after 1570 (unlikely on the ground of the history and construction of the instrument), or b) the label was inserted after 1570 (perhaps even after 1892; see the remarks concerning the Hajdecki lira da braccio, below). In any case, the label must have been inserted after Giovanni Maria's demise since he was certainly dead long before 1570. But the posthumous insertion of the label does not necessarily show that the lira da braccio is not by Giovanni Maria. Among other things, the original label may have been lost and simply replaced at a later time.

The lira da braccio as a species was one of the principal ancestors of the violin. The lira da braccio in the Hill Collection, although smaller than usual, is one of the most beautiful in existence. It is in a perfect state of preservation. The outlines of the body, particularly when viewed from the side, are remarkably close to those of the violin. Observe also the short and fat neck, similar to that of the violin. The tuning was d d' for the two strings running off the fingerboard, g g' d' a' d'' (or e' ') for the stopped strings.[1]

The lira da braccio in the Hill Collection—or its twin—must have been owned at one time by Major Alexander Hajdecki, and it was from a careful study of his instrument that Hajdecki formulated the important and generally accepted theory about the relation of the lira da braccio to the early violin (see his *Die italienische Lira da braccio,* Mostar, 1892). In the course of his book, Hajdecki describes the instrument he possessed, giving the label and the dimensions. The latter are the same as those of the lira da braccio in the Hill Collection but the labels differ, that of the Hajdecki lira da braccio reading (Hajdecki, p. 6):

> Gaspard Duiffopruggar [*sic*]
> Bononiensis anno 1515

[1] For an excellent article, see Emanuel Winternitz, "Lira da braccio" in *Die Musik in Geschichte und Gegenwart,* viii (Cassell, 1960).

This label is certainly a forgery since Duiffoprugcar (the preferred spelling; the German form is Tieffenbrucker) was not born until 1514.

How the lira da braccio came into the hands of the Hills is not known.

Hill Gift, 1939.                                        *Annual Report*, 1939, p. 27.

| MEASUREMENTS | *Inches* | *Millimetres* |
|---|---|---|
| Length overall | $25\frac{1}{2}$ | 647 |
| Length of body | $15\frac{1}{4}$ | 387 |
| Width, upper bouts | $7\frac{3}{8}$ | 187 |
| Width, centre bouts | $5\frac{5}{16}$ | 135 |
| Width, lower bouts | $9\frac{3}{16}$ | 234 |
| Depth of sides | $1\frac{5}{16}$ (full) | 34 |
| Length of fingerboard | $7\frac{11}{16}$ | 196 |
| String length | $12\frac{3}{4}$ | 323 |

# 9 (D. 2:2) LIRA-VIOLA by Gasparo da Salò, Brescia, 1561.

Plate 9 (a, b, c)

Label:                          Gasparo da Salò, in Brescia
                                                1561

This instrument has four strings tuned like a modern viola. It is essentially an alto violin with no middle bouts, and it has the indented base at the tailpiece characteristic of the lira da braccio. Thus our lira-viola is a hybrid form, found during the early evolution of the violin family and combining elements of the viola and the lira da braccio. It is capable of producing a beautiful tone of considerable power; and it must have been made when Gasparo was a young man of twenty-one, just after he arrived in Brescia from Salò. Gasparo da Salò did not invent the violin, as is often said; nor was he the first famous maker (see the remarks to No. 10).

The table of the lira-viola is made of the same curiously latticed wood (cedar of Lebanon) noted in the descriptions of the bass viol and cittern by the same maker (see No. 2 and No. 31). The colour is golden-brown. The f-holes are typical of Brescian sound holes and those of this maker. The two-piece back and ribs are made of handsomely figured maple. There is double purfling, front and back. The head and neck of this instrument are not original but have been restored in the old style (note particularly the old form of the scroll). The tailpiece and fingerboard are also not original. From the d'Este Collection.

Hill Gift, 1939.

| MEASUREMENTS | Inches | Millimetres |
|---|---|---|
| Length overall | $25\frac{3}{4}$ | 655 |
| Length of body | $16\frac{1}{2}$ | 420 |
| Width, upper bouts | $8\frac{3}{8}$ | 213 |
| Width, centre bouts | $6\frac{1}{4}$ | 158 |
| Width, lower bouts | $10\frac{3}{16}$ | 258 |
| Depth of sides | $1\frac{1}{2}$ | 38 |
| Length of fingerboard | $9\frac{1}{2}$ | 241 |
| String length | $13\frac{7}{8}$ | 353 |

# 10 (D. 8:2) VIOLIN ('Charles IX') by Andrea Amati, Cremona, 1564.

Plate 10 (a, b, c)

Label:           (top line cannot be deciphered)
                  Cremona MDLXIV

This is a small violin, about a half-inch shorter than the modern instrument, one of a set made for Charles IX of France by Andrea Amati (born not later than 1511; died about 1580). The royal insignia used by Charles IX and also by his mother, Catherine de' Medici, is painted on the back and ribs. Only part of the original insignia is still visible, including fragments of the motto *Pietate et Iustitia* [Iusticia?] on the ribs. Andrea Amati, the founder of the Amati dynasty and the Cremona school of violin making, was probably the first *famous* maker of violins.

The table is made of open-grain pine, varnished a golden-brown, there being some discoloration on the left side of the tailpiece. The one-piece back and the ribs are maple of a handsome figure, and the f-holes are characteristic of the maker. The ivory tailpiece and the saddle have been renewed. The pegbox and scroll are original but the neck, fingerboard, and tailpiece are not.

This extraordinary violin is one of the oldest in existence and one of the best preserved. The tone is remarkably mellow and powerful. This instrument and its companion viola (No. 11) must have been used constantly by French musicians at the French court, especially on such famous occasions as the performance of the *Ballet comique de la reine* (1581). Of the thirty-eight instruments of the violin family said to have been commissioned by Charles IX from Andrea Amati, this and No. 11 are among the few still remaining. However, another violin of the same set (and practically identical but dated 1574) is now in the City Museum of Carlisle (formerly in the Mounsey-Heysham Collection). Another, of the same date, formerly in private hands in New York, has now, after nearly four centuries, been returned to

Cremona, the city of its birth. Most of the others were apparently destroyed during the course of the French Revolution (for further information on this set of thirty-eight instruments, see David D. Boyden, *The History of Violin Playing*, London, 1965).

Hill Gift, 1939.                                   *Annual Report*, 1939, p. 27.

| MEASUREMENTS | Inches | Millimetres |
|---|---|---|
| Length overall | $22\frac{5}{8}$ | 574 |
| Length of body | $13\frac{7}{16}$ | 342 |
| Width, upper bouts | $6\frac{1}{4}$ | 159 |
| Width, centre bouts | $4\frac{3}{16}$ | 107 |
| Width, lower bouts | $7\frac{3}{4}$ | 196 |
| Depth of sides | $1\frac{1}{8}$ | 28·5 |
| Length of fingerboard | 9 | 228 |
| String length | $12\frac{1}{2}$ | 317 |

## 11 (D. 8:1) VIOLA ('Charles IX') by Andrea Amati, Cremona, 1574.
Plate 11 (a, b, c)
Label:                          Andrea Amadi [*sic*] in
                                 Cremona M.D.LXXiiij

This very large (tenor) viola, tuned as a regular viola but intended for its deeper registers, is one of the few remaining instruments of the set made by Andrea Amati for Charles IX of France (see remarks to No. 10 above). It also bears the royal insignia and motto, rather more of which is preserved than in No. 10. This is a magnificent instrument in a perfect state of preservation with a beautiful tone of extraordinary depth. The table is made of pine of varying grain, varnished a rich golden-brown colour, the two-piece back, sides, and head being of small-figured maple. The pegbox and scroll, but not the pegs, are original. The tailpiece is probably original but not the fingerboard or the neck. The latter, however, has been restored in old style. The bass bar and sound post are modern. The curious, worn-down flattening at the back of the scroll (Pl. 11c) came about from sliding the instrument into a case.

This instrument was bought between 1920 and 1925 in the Hague from Vedral, previously having belonged to a convent, name and place unknown.

Hill Gift, 1939.                                   *Annual Report*, 1939, p. 27.

| MEASUREMENTS | Inches | Millimetres |
|---|---|---|
| Length overall | $29\frac{1}{2}$ | 750 |
| Length of body | $18\frac{1}{2}$ | 470 |
| Width, upper bouts | 9 | 229 |
| Width, centre bouts | $6\frac{3}{16}$ | 157 |
| Width, lower bouts | $10\frac{5}{8}$ | 270 |
| Depth of sides | $1\frac{1}{2}$–$1\frac{5}{8}$ | 38–40 |
| Length of fingerboard | 11 | 279 |
| String length | $15\frac{7}{8}$ | 403 |

# 12 (D. 2:4) VIOLA by Gasparo da Salò, Brescia, late 16th century.

Plate 12 (a, b, c)

Label:           Gasparo da Salò, in Brescia [no date]

The table is made of pine of fine grain, varnished a golden-brown colour. The two-piece back of figured maple is cut on the quarter, while the sides, marked by a wavy curl, are cut on the slab. The sound holes of normal f-form, although rather long, are typical of Brescian makers and also of Gasparo da Salò. Single purfling is used.

This instrument has its original neck (Pl. 12b), which is very short ($4\frac{7}{8}$ inches). Similarly, the inlaid fingerboard, inlaid tailpiece, pegbox, and scroll are original. The bridge, the pegs, and the ivory nut are not.

This is a large (tenor) viola; and, like the 'Charles IX' Amati, of deep, mellow tone, perhaps of greater carrying power. Few violas have survived from the sixteenth century and of these, still fewer of large size have retained their original dimensions (like this and the 'Charles IX' Amati viola), since a number of them were later cut down to a more manageable size.

Hill Gift, 1939.

| MEASUREMENTS | Inches | Millimetres |
|---|---|---|
| Length overall | $27\frac{1}{2}$ | 697 |
| Length of body | $17\frac{1}{2}$ | 444 |
| Width, upper bouts | $8\frac{9}{16}$ | 218 |
| Width, centre bouts | $5\frac{3}{4}$ | 147 |
| Width, lower bouts | $10\frac{1}{8}$ | 258 |
| Depth of sides | $1\frac{1}{2}$ | 38 |
| Length of fingerboard | $8\frac{1}{2}$ | 215 |
| String length | $14\frac{1}{4}$ | 368 |

**13** (D. 8:6) VIOLA by Antonius and Hieronymus (the 'brothers') Amati, Cremona, 1592.
Plate 13 (a, b, c)
Label:  Antonius & Hieronymus Fr. Amati
Cremonen Andreae fil. F. 1592

The table is made of pine of undistinguished irregular grain, golden-brown in colour, while the two-piece back and the sides are of small-figured maple, varnished a warm golden-brown. The head is made of plainer wood. This viola bears the brand of the Medici on the fluting of the head and also the initial 'M' (cf. No. 7) on the button of the back (Pl. 13c). The head and the tailpiece are original; and although the pegs, the neck, and fingerboard are not original, they have been restored in old style. The makers, the 'brothers Amati', are the second generation of the family, being the sons of Andrea Amati (cf. the remarks to No. 7 and No. 10).

This viola, made originally for the Medici family, was formerly the property of Sir William Hamilton, who acquired this fine instrument in the late eighteenth century when he was ambassador at Naples (letter from Alfred Hill, 1 June 1937).

Hill Gift, 1939.                              *Annual Report*, 1939, p. 27.

| MEASUREMENTS | Inches | Millimetres |
|---|---|---|
| Length overall | $28\frac{1}{2}$ | 725 |
| Length of body | $17\frac{7}{8}$ | 454 |
| Width, upper bouts | $8\frac{5}{8}$ | 220 |
| Width, centre bouts | 6 | 152 |
| Width, lower bouts | $10\frac{1}{2}$ | 266 |
| Depth of sides | $1\frac{1}{2}$–$1\frac{9}{16}$ | 38–40 |
| Length of fingerboard | 11 | 279 |
| String length | $15\frac{1}{2}$ | 394 |

**14** (D. 8:4) VIOLIN by Antonius & Hieronymus Amati, Cremona, 1618.
Plate 14 (a, b, c)
Label:  Antonius, & Hieronymus Fr. Amati
Cremon Andreae fil. F. 1618

This small violin (13-inch body), an inch shorter than the normal violin, was probably intended for a child. The table is made of open-grain pine, varnished a golden-brown. The f-holes are typical. The beautiful two-piece back (in perfect condition), sides, and head are made of handsomely figured maple, the varnish being a light golden-brown colour. The head and pegbox are original, but the neck, fingerboard, and tailpiece are modern.

Presented in 1948 by Mr. A. Phillips Hill in accordance with the wishes of the late Arthur and Alfred Hill.

*Annual Report*, 1948, p. 45.

| MEASUREMENTS | Inches | Millimetres |
|---|---|---|
| Length overall | $21\frac{7}{8}$ | 555 |
| Length of body | $13\frac{1}{16}$ | 331 |
| Width, upper bouts | 6 | 153 |
| Width, centre bouts | $4\frac{1}{8}$ | 104 |
| Width, lower bouts | $7\frac{7}{16}$ | 189 |
| Depth of sides | $1\frac{1}{16}$ | 27 |
| Length of fingerboard | $9\frac{1}{2}$ | 241 |
| String length | $12\frac{3}{16}$ | 310 |

# 15 (D. 8:3) VIOLIN ('Alard') by Nicola Amati (1596–1684), Cremona, 1649.
Plate 15 (a, b, c)

Label:  Nicolaus Amatus Cremonen. Hieronymi
Fil. ac Antonij Nepos, Fecit 1649

With this splendid instrument, we reach the third generation of the Amati family, Nicola being the son of Girolamo (Hieronymus), the younger of the 'brothers'. Nicola is generally considered to be the greatest of all the Amatis, the model and inspiration of many following generations. Nicola Amati was probably the teacher of Antonio Stradivari, although this cannot be proved.

The table of this violin is made of pine of even, open grain, varnished a golden-brown. The table is rather worn on both sides of the tailpiece, pointing to considerable use (before the advent of the chin-rest about 1820, the violinist rested his chin directly on the wood, originally to the right of the tailpiece and later to the left). The f-holes are beautifully modelled and cut. The two-piece back, sides, and head are made of strikingly handsome figured maple, varnished a rich golden brown. The middle of the back is arched very high. The neck is original although it has been lengthened, and one can still see traces of marks of the original nail holes visible on the heel of the old neck. The pegbox and scroll are original. The latter is beautifully cut—in fact, it is one of Amati's finest heads. The fingerboard, pegs, and tailpiece are modern.

This violin was formerly the property of the celebrated violinist, Delphin Alard (1815–88). (See also No. 18 below for Alard's ownership of the 'Messiah' violin by Stradivari.)

Presented in 1948 by Mr. A. Phillips Hill in accordance with the wishes of the late Arthur and Alfred Hill.

*Annual Report*, 1948, p. 45.

| MEASUREMENTS | Inches | Millimetres |
|---|---|---|
| Length overall | 23 | 583 |
| Length of body | 13 $\frac{13}{16}$ | 351 |
| Width, upper bouts | 6 $\frac{7}{16}$ | 163 |
| Width, centre bouts | 4 $\frac{3}{8}$ | 111 |
| Width, lower bouts | 8 | 203 |
| Depth of sides | 1 $\frac{5}{32}$ | 29 |
| Length of fingerboard | 10 $\frac{5}{16}$ | 262 |
| String length | 12 $\frac{15}{16}$ | 328 |

# 16 VIOLIN by Jacob Stainer, Absam in Tyrol, 1672.

Plate 16 (a, b, c)

Label: almost illegible; only the date—1672—can be deciphered. Stainer's labels are generally worded as follows:

Jacobus Stainer in Absam Prope Oenipontum 16 . . . (sometimes the word 'Fecit' is included before the date).

The table is made of even and rather open grain; the varnish is worn on both sides of the tailpiece (cf. remarks to No. 15). The back is in one piece, but narrow 'wings' have been inserted on both sides of the lower bouts. The ribs are made of a faintly figured wood, and the head of plain wood. The scroll is original, but the pegbox, neck, fingerboard, and tailpiece are not. The highly arched modelling and f-holes are similar to those of Nicola Amati's violins.

In the Stainers and Amatis, the seventeenth century reached a high point in violin making (however, this particular Stainer is not nearly as distinguished an instrument as the 'Alard' Amati). Instruments by these makers were held in the same esteem in their day as the Stradivaris and Guarneris are now—a situation that prevailed until Viotti appeared in Paris with his Stradivari about 1780, starting a demand for these instruments that has never subsided.

This Stainer violin was not part of the Hill Gift but was bequeathed by Rev. E. C. Tippetts in 1957.

*Annual Report*, 1957, p. 46.

| MEASUREMENTS | *Inches* | *Millimetres* |
|---|---|---|
| Length overall | 23 1/16 | 585 |
| Length of body | 13 15/16 | 353 |
| Width, upper bouts | 6 9/16 | 167 |
| Width, centre bouts | 4 5/16 | 110 |
| Width, lower bouts | 8 1/8 | 206 |
| Depth of sides | 1 1/8–1 3/16 | 28–30 |
| Length of fingerboard | 10 1/2 | 267 |
| String length | 12 3/4 | 323 |

# 17 (D. 8:5) VIOLIN (inlaid) by Antonio Stradivari (1644?–1737), Cremona, 1683.

Plate 17 (a, b, c)

Label:                    Antonius Stradiuarius Cremonensis
                         Faciebat Anno 1683

This violin is an early example of Stradivari's work, a beautifully inlaid violin of small pattern, perhaps for a child, and if so, for a beloved or wealthy one. The table, of even grain with golden varnish, is worn at both sides of the tailpiece (cf. remarks to No. 15). The back is made in one piece of handsomely figured maple. The golden varnish is rubbed at base and shoulders. The purfling of the table and back is carried out with inlays of ivory diamond-shapes. The button at the top of the back (Pl. 17c) is made of mother-of-pearl in a flower design of eight petals. The sides of slightly figured maple are covered by floral decorations, the latter not being painted on, but inlaid with black mastic, an extraordinary feat of craftsmanship. After 1690 such floral designs are usually painted on by Stradivari. The pegbox and scroll are decorated with the same motifs as the ribs and similarly inlaid with black mastic. The original neck has been lengthened to modern standards (two nail-holes are visible; cf. remarks to No. 15). The fingerboard and tailpiece, although they carry out the motifs of the original decorative inlay, are modern. (For other examples of inlaid Stradivari violins, see *Antonio Stradivari, His Life and Works (1644–1737)* by W. Henry Hill, Arthur F. Hill, & Alfred E. Hill, London, 1902.)

Until 1690 (or thereabouts) Stradivari's violins were under the influence of Nicola Amati, and are often called *Amatisé*. In this instrument the Amati influence may perhaps be seen in the rather arched table, although the back is somewhat flat.

This inlaid Stradivari violin was bought from the d'Este family by Cipriani Potter. The Hills bought the violin from Potter at the end of the nineteenth century.

(For the disputed birthdate of Stradivari, see David D. Boyden, *The History of Violin Playing*, London, 1965, Appendix.)

Hill Gift (Supplementary Item), 1946.  *Annual Report*, 1946, p. 29.

| MEASUREMENTS | Inches | Millimetres |
|---|---|---|
| Length overall | $22\frac{5}{8}$ | 575 |
| Length of body | $13\frac{3}{16}$ | 340 |
| Width, upper bouts | $6\frac{1}{32}$ | 153 |
| Width, centre bouts | $4\frac{7}{32}$ | 107 |
| Width, lower bouts | $7\frac{9}{16}$ | 192 |
| Depth of sides | $1\frac{3}{16}-1\frac{1}{4}$ | 30–31·7 |
| Length of fingerboard | $8\frac{3}{4}$ | 222 |
| String length | $12\frac{1}{2}$ | 318 |

# 18 (D. 3:1) VIOLIN ('Le Messie') by Antonio Stradivari, Cremona, 1716.

Plate 18 (a, b, c, d, e, f and Frontispiece)
Label:              Antonius Stradiuarius Cremonensis
                    Faciebat Anno 1716

This is one of the most famous violins in the world, and one of the most celebrated of all Stradivari's instruments, from the 'golden' period of his production. It is in practically mint condition, and from its appearance one gets an idea of the fresh and glowing colours of these violins in their youth. The table is varnished a light orange-brown, fine grain in the centre, the grain opening somewhat on the flanks. The back in two pieces is made of handsomely figured curl, somewhat irregular in pattern. The varnish is slightly chipped at the centre. The beautiful scroll and pegbox are outlined by a blackened bevel (Pl. 18d, e). The neck is original but it has been lengthened to modern measurement and tilted back as is customary today. The fingerboard is modern.

Vuillaume, who owned this instrument at one time (see below), fitted the tailpiece and pegs that are now on the violin. He also removed the bass bar, and put in a longer and stronger one. Later, the Hills put in a still stronger one, which is there now. Vuillaume, however, had saved the original bass bar, which has been recovered and is now displayed with the violin. The original bass bar was presented to the Museum by Mr. A. Phillips Hill in 1956.

The 'Messiah' violin follows generally the model that Stradivari created with the 'Betts' violin of 1704, but it has its own pronounced individuality, shown in such details as the exceptionally square corners (Pl. 18a), the slant of the f-holes, and the sharply rising ridge of the table. The 'Messiah' was also the model for many imitations, the most notable of which were the work of the great French maker, Vuillaume.

How does it happen that an instrument two hundred and fifty years old has been so perfectly preserved? For one thing, it has hardly ever been played; and to explain this, one must relate the story of its past. When Stradivari died in 1737, aged over ninety, there were ninety-one instruments in his workshop. Nearly forty years later, in 1775, there were still ten instruments in the possession of Paolo Stradivari, the youngest child of Antonio's second marriage. Among these ten was the 'Messiah', a name acquired later. In 1775 Paolo contracted to sell these instruments and other things from his father's shop to Count Cozio di Salabue, one of the most important collectors in history; and, although Paolo died before the transaction was concluded, Salabue acquired the instruments. Salabue kept the 'Messiah' until 1827, when he sold it to Luigi Tarisio, a fascinating character who, from small beginnings, built up an important business dealing in violins. However, Tarisio could not bear to part with this particular instrument. Instead, he made it a favourite topic of conversation, and he intrigued dealers on his visits to Paris with accounts of this marvellous 'Salabue' violin, as it was then called, taking care, however, never to bring it with him. One day Tarisio was discoursing to Vuillaume on the merits of this unknown and marvellous instrument, when the violinist Delphin Alard, who was present, exclaimed: 'Then your violin is like the Messiah: one always expects him but he never appears' ('Ah ça, votre violon est donc comme le Messie: on l'attend toujours, et il ne parait jamais'). Thus the violin was baptized with the name by which it is still known today.

Tarisio never parted with the violin and not until his death in 1854 had anyone outside Italy seen it. In 1855, Vuillaume was able to acquire it, and it remained with him, also until his death. Vuillaume guarded the 'Messiah' jealously, keeping it in a glass case and allowing no one to examine it. However, he did allow it to be shown at the 1872 Exhibition of Instruments in the South Kensington Museum, and this was its first appearance in England. After Vuillaume's death in 1875, the violin became the property of his two daughters and then of his son-in-law, the violinist, Alard. After Alard's death in 1888, his heirs sold the 'Messiah' in 1890 to W. E. Hill and Sons on behalf of Mr. R. Crawford of Edinburgh for £2,000, at that time the largest sum ever paid for a violin.

In 1904 it was repurchased by the Hills, who also became much attached to this violin, and not until 1913 could they be induced to sell it, this time to Mr. Richard Bennett who was forming a fine collection of Cremona instruments. Mr. Bennett did not play on these instruments but he seems to have derived considerable pleasure from the process of admiring them. In 1928, because of his failing health, Mr. Bennett returned his whole collection to the Hills, and Mr. Arthur and Mr. Alfred Hill decided to present the 'Messiah' violin, together with other fine Italian instruments, to the nation.

It is sometimes said that the 'Messiah' violin owes its preservation in mint condition to the fact that no one wanted to play it, the tone being not particularly distinguished. We can give the lie to this gossip by quoting a very interesting letter in the possession of the Ashmolean Museum. It is dated 31 March 1891, and was written by a famous violinist to Mr. Crawford of Edinburgh who, as explained above, acquired the violin in 1890. This letter is worth quoting in full:

Dear Mr. Crawford,
    I received your kind note, and it is a great pleasure to be reminded of the most pleasant hour I had the privilege of spending in your house, surrounded by the treasures in your picture gallery and playing your splendid fiddles. Of course, the sound of *the* Strad, that *unique* 'Messie' turns up again and again in my memory, with its combined sweetness and grandeur, that struck me so much in hearing it. It is indeed justly celebrated, and I hope I may again put my bow to it some day. But I long to see the second Strad and the Guarnerius again too.
    Believe me, dear Mr. Crawford to be with kindest regards
                                    Yours most sincerely,
                                    (signed) Joseph Joachim

(For a special study of this violin, see W. E. Hill & Sons, *The Salabue Stradivari*, London, 1891.)

Hill Gift, 1940.

*Annual Report*, 1939, p. 27 (where its reception is forecast; its arrival in 1940 and its immediate removal to safety were not recorded publicly).

| MEASUREMENTS | Inches | Millimetres |
|---|---|---|
| Length overall | $23\frac{3}{8}$ | 593 |
| Length of body | 14 | 356 |
| Width, upper bouts | $6\frac{5}{8}$ | 168 |
| Width, centre bouts | $4\frac{7}{16}$ | 112 |
| Width, lower bouts | $8\frac{3}{16}$ | 213 |
| Depth of sides | $1\frac{1}{4}$–$1\frac{5}{32}$ | 29–32 |
| Length of fingerboard | $10\frac{1}{2}$ | 267 |
| String length | 13 | 330 |

# THE BOWS

Makers of the bows are unknown except as noted. The dates given are estimated on the basis of the shape of the bow stick, the type of bow head, the type of frog, and the screw button. However, the uncertainty involved in dating bows means that an error of ten, twenty, or even more years must be allowed for any given bow.

Describing the heads of the bows brings up a problem of terminology. So little has been written about the evolution of the early bow that no real need has been felt previously for terms to describe the various types of bow heads involved in the change from the early bow to the modern type standardized by François Tourte in the 1780s.[1] The earliest of our bows (Nos. 19–21) have heads typical of the time, called 'pike's head', characteristically with a pointed bill (cf. the plates). In bows Nos. 22–23, the bill is shortened and modified—hence the name 'modified pike's head'. With bow No. 24 a change in the shape and substance of the head is discernible, a change that will lead to the modern Tourte bow. Bows Nos. 24–28 are all transitional types. No. 24 anticipates the hatchet-head shape of No. 25 and No. 27, themselves both transitional bows. No. 26 and No. 28 show vestiges of the old pike bill and, at the same time, anticipate in the substance and shape of the head the modern Tourte model, illustrated by bows Nos. 29–30.

The following twelve bows were presented in 1948 by Mr. A. Phillips Hill in accordance with the wishes of the late Arthur and Alfred Hill.

*Annual Report*, 1948, p. 45.

19 VIOLIN BOW, slot-notch (or clip-in) type, *c.* 1700.
Plate 19 (a, b)

This handsome, slightly convex, bow stick of snakewood is fluted part-way above the frog, the latter also being made of snakewood. Light in weight, the bow is

---

[1] One solution is to call all early bows 'Corelli bows', but this term does not allow for the marked differences of individual early bows, nor has anyone defined what a 'Corelli bow' is. Actually, we do not know precisely what kind of a bow Corelli used.

beautifully balanced. The graceful pike's head ends in a slender bill. The bow hair is kept at fixed tension by the clip-in piece of wood that snaps into a slot in the bow stick (Pl. 19b). The end of the stick is immovable; it is not a screw button to regulate a movable nut, as one might suppose from the light fluting around the end of the stick. Examples of clip-in bows are rare, and this particular bow is one of the best in existence as regards beauty of workmanship and excellence of playing qualities.

| MEASUREMENTS | Inches | Millimetres | | Ounces | Grams |
|---|---|---|---|---|---|
| Length overall | $27\frac{11}{16}$ | 704 | Weight | $1\frac{3}{4}$ | 51 |
| Length of playing hair | 22 | 559 | | | |

## 20 BASS-VIOL BOW.                    c. 1740–50
Plate 20

This snakewood bow is strongly constructed and massive in appearance. It is fluted in the upper two-thirds of its length, presumably to maintain strength while reducing weight and increasing flexibility. The camber is slightly concave when unstrung. Other features are a pike's head of heavy construction and a movable frog of ivory, regulated by an ivory screw button.

| MEASUREMENTS | Inches | Millimetres | | Ounces | Grams |
|---|---|---|---|---|---|
| Length overall | $28\frac{15}{16}$ | 735 | Weight | $2\frac{1}{2}$ | 72 |
| Length of playing hair | $23\frac{5}{8}$ | 601 | | | |

## 21 BASS-VIOL BOW by Peter Walmsley (or Wamsley), working 1720–44.
Plate 21 (a, b)

This snakewood bow stick is still heavier in construction than No. 20. It is fluted through its whole length, but the type of fluting in the lower third differs from that in the upper two-thirds. The camber of the bow stick is slightly convex. The massive pike's head exhibits a very long bill. The ivory nut is stamped on both sides with the maker's name: WAMSLEY—a very rare occurrence before 1750 (Pl. 21b). The ivory end-tip appears to be a screw button, but it is not movable, and the frog is actually a clip-in wedge to tighten the hair, as in No. 19. Like the latter, No. 21 is also a rare example of a clip-in bow. Note that the 'snow-plough' front edge of the clip-in (where it snaps into place; see Pl. 21b) was retained on bows after the frog had become movable and after this feature of the clip-in had ceased to be functional.

| MEASUREMENTS | Inches | Millimetres | | | Ounces | Grams |
|---|---|---|---|---|---|---|
| Length overall | $29\frac{7}{8}$ | 760 | | Weight | $2\frac{7}{8}$ | 82 |
| Length of playing hair | $23\frac{1}{8}$ | 588 | | | | |

# 22 VIOLA BOW by Thomas Smith (working *c.* 1756), pupil of Walmsley.
Plate 22

The bow stick of snakewood follows much the same design as No. 21, including the fluting in the upper two-thirds of the stick, the decorative design in the lower third, and the ivory frog and ivory screw button; and it is likely that 'T. Smith', the maker, was working to a model of 'Walmsley', his master. However, No. 22 is much lighter in weight and construction than No. 21, the bow stick being smaller in diameter, and the bow head shorter and much less massive—a modified pike's head. Another interesting feature is that No. 22 has a greater length of playing hair than No. 21, but, at the same time, a shorter overall length.

While No. 22 is related to No. 21 in decoration and design, it has also a kinship to No. 19 with respect to silhouette and head. However, in this case, No. 19 is still lighter in construction than No. 22.

The ivory frog of No. 22 resembles that of No. 21 (and it resembles No. 19 still more in design and profile); but unlike Nos. 19 and 21, No. 22 has a movable frog, not a clip-in, and is regulated by an ivory screw button (but note that No. 22 still retains the 'snow-plough'; cf. remarks to No. 21). The ivory of the frog has yellowed markedly, especially on one side, and the name T. SMITH can be seen (although not easily) stamped on both sides of the frog.

| MEASUREMENTS | Inches | Millimetres | | | Ounces | Grams |
|---|---|---|---|---|---|---|
| Length overall | $28\frac{3}{4}$ | 730 | | Weight | $2\frac{1}{8}$ | 60 |
| Length of playing hair | $23\frac{11}{16}$ | 602 | | | | |

# 23 VIOLIN BOW                          *c.* 1740
Plate 23

The concave bow stick of snakewood is fluted in the upper two-thirds of its length, being octagonal in the lower third. The modified pike's head is rather massive in appearance (cf. No. 19), although not ungraceful. A movable frog of ebony (?) and a screw button of ivory are additional features.

| MEASUREMENTS | Inches | Millimetres | | | Ounces | Grams |
|---|---|---|---|---|---|---|
| Length overall | $27\frac{5}{8}$ | 702 | | Weight | $2\frac{1}{16}$ | 58 |
| Length of playing hair | $23\frac{7}{16}$ | 595 | | | | |

# 24 VIOLIN BOW                                               c. 1750
Plate 24

The rather thin bow stick of dark pernambuco wood is unfluted and slightly concave in camber. Green-yellow windings are used immediately above the frog. The
latter, exceptionally short, slight, and made of ivory, is movable and regulated by
an ivory screw button. The bow head, a transitional type on the way to the later
'hatchet' head (cf. No. 25 and No. 27), still retains the vestige of the bill of the older
pike's head, a delicate and graceful construction.

   According to Desmond Hill, this bow once bore a label stating that it was supplied
by Richard Duke but was the work of Edward Dodd.

| MEASUREMENTS | Inches | Millimetres | | Ounces | Grams |
|---|---|---|---|---|---|
| Length overall | $28\frac{3}{4}$ | 730 | Weight | $1\frac{5}{8}$ | 46 |
| Length of playing hair | $23\frac{11}{16}$ | 620 | | | |

# 25 VIOLIN BOW                                               c. 1750
Plate 25 (a, b)

The concave bow stick of pernambuco wood is concave and unfluted. Windings of
darkish green thread are used at the lower part of the bow stick above the frog. The
hatchet head (Pl. 25a) is characteristic of bows just prior to the advent of the modern
(Tourte) design. The ivory frog of curious, ornamental shape (Pl. 25b) has no ferrule
and no slide to discipline its narrow ribbon of hair. However, the frog is movable
and regulated by an ivory screw button with knob flattened on both sides. Just
above the screw button, the sides and top of the bow stick are ornamented for a
short length with ivory inlay (Pl. 25b).

| MEASUREMENTS | Inches | Millimetres | | Ounces | Grams |
|---|---|---|---|---|---|
| Length overall | 28 | 711 | Weight | $1\frac{3}{4}$ | 52 |
| Length of playing hair | $24\frac{13}{16}$ | 631 | | | |

# 26 VIOLIN BOW by Tourte père (father of François Tourte), c. 1760.
Plate 26 (a, b)

The bow stick of pernambuco wood is concave of pronounced camber, fluted in
the upper two-thirds of its length. The bow head is a high and massive one. It

anticipates the modern Tourte design in substance and form while still retaining vestiges of the pike's head. The bow stick is wound at the frog with green thread interspersed with four bands of dark silver. The frog is a new shape, compared with bows previously described, being squared-off in appearance. The movable frog is regulated by an ivory screw button. The bow hair is slightly wider (Pl. 26b) than in earlier bows, but there is no ferrule and no slide.

| MEASUREMENTS | Inches | Millimetres | | Ounces | Grams |
|---|---|---|---|---|---|
| Length overall | $29\frac{1}{16}$ | 738 | Weight | $1\frac{11}{16}$ | 49 |
| Length of playing hair | $25\frac{5}{16}$ | 644 | | | |

# 27 VIOLIN BOW by Edward Dodd (c. 1705–1810)    c. 1775
Plate 27

No. 27 is the first of three 'Dodd' violin bows (Pls. 27, 28, 29)—this one being by Edward Dodd and the two following by his son, John, often called 'the English Tourte'. It is very instructive to see the evolution of these bows, one to the other, especially in the details of the bow heads and the frogs.

As is common with Dodd bows, No. 27 is stamped with the name of the maker, and in this bow DODD is stamped on both the bow stick and the ivory frog. The cylindrical bow stick is concave in camber, and the pernambuco-wood is a beautiful golden-brown. The hatchet head, massive and rather clumsily executed, suggests that this is the earliest of the three Dodd bows and that the maker was Edward, the father. The face of the bow tip is ivory. The movable ivory frog is regulated by an ivory screw button. The hair is still a narrow ribbon, without ferrule or slide, and this, too, indicates an early Dodd bow.

| MEASUREMENTS | Inches | Millimetres | | Ounces | Grams |
|---|---|---|---|---|---|
| Length overall | $28\frac{7}{8}$ | 734 | Weight | $1\frac{11}{16}$ | 48 |
| Length of playing hair | $24\frac{13}{16}$ | 628 | | | |

# 28 VIOLIN BOW by John Dodd (1752–1835)    c. 1780
Plate 28

Like No. 27, this bow is stamped DODD on the bow stick. The latter is slightly concave, fluted throughout, and made of pernambuco wood (similar to No. 26). The bow stick has a worn place at the lowest extremity (next to the frog), where it has been gripped by the player's thumb, showing that the hand was held in the lowest possible position. The head is a massive transitional type similar to No. 26, retaining vestiges of the old pike's-head bill but closer to the modern Tourte design. Mother-of-pearl is inset into the ebony face of the head, giving a handsome ornamental effect. The ebony frog has also a diamond-shaped mother-of-pearl inlay in the centre. An important new feature is the ferrule at the hair-end of the frog, making the hair lie uniformly in a flat ribbon (cf. Pl. 29b). The hair is also wider than in previous bows. The hair along the face of the frog is covered with a mother-of-pearl slide (cf. Pl. 29b). The frog is movable and regulated by a silver screw button. The latter now assumes the new squared-off shape at its end, it is rounded, and it is made of silver with a black band. The end-tip of the screw button is also ornamented with mother-of-pearl set in a black border.

| MEASUREMENTS | Inches | Millimetres | | Ounces | Grams |
|---|---|---|---|---|---|
| Length overall | 29 | 737 | Weight | $1\frac{11}{16}$ | 49 |
| Length of playing hair | $25\frac{1}{4}$ | 641 | | | |

## 29 VIOLIN BOW by John Dodd     c. 1800
Plate 29 (a, b, c, d)

Like No. 27 and No. 28, this bow is stamped DODD on the bow stick and the frog (Pl. 29d). This is a fully developed modern bow, closely resembling the model standardized by François Tourte in the 1780s, being a cylindrical bow stick of concave camber, made of pernambuco wood, golden-brown in colour but a bit deeper in tone than No. 27. Windings of green-yellow thread cover the bow stick at the frog. The head, a fully developed modern (Tourte) design, is beautifully cut. The face of the head, like that of No. 28, is ebony with a mother-of-pearl inset (Pl. 29c). The frog is similar to that of No. 28, being made of ebony with mother-of-pearl inlay in the centre (but circular design in this case). The hair, of modern width, is flattened by a ferrule and is covered by a mother-of-pearl slide (Pl. 29b), which is carried around the end of the frog and up its back to the bow stick. The silver screw button (which regulates the movable frog) and the end of the screw-tip are both decorated with mother-of-pearl set in a black border, as in No. 28.

| MEASUREMENTS | Inches | Millimetres | | Ounces | Grams |
|---|---|---|---|---|---|
| Length overall | $28\frac{3}{4}$ | 730 | Weight | $1\frac{3}{4}$ | 53 |
| Length of playing hair | $24\frac{13}{16}$ | 631 | | | |

# 30 VIOLIN BOW                          c. 1820
Plate 30 (a, b)

This Tourte-model bow of German origin is the standard (modern) shape and size, slightly longer than No. 29. The concave bow stick of pernambuco wood is octagonal. Silver and green threads are used as windings on the bow stick at the frog (Pl. 30b). The head is modelled on the modern (Tourte) design.

Gold and mother-of-pearl are used extensively in this bow. Gold covers the face of the head, and inlaid designs of mother-of-pearl and gold decorate the frog and the portion of the bow stick above the frog (Pl. 30b). Gold is used for the ferrule, mother-of-pearl for the slide, and gold for an end-piece band that is carried from the end of the slide around the end of the frog and part way toward the bow stick. The screw button that regulates the movable frog is ornamented with gold and mother-of-pearl. Altogether, it is a handsome bow, although rather profusely decorated.

| MEASUREMENTS | Inches | Millimetres | | Ounces | Grams |
|---|---|---|---|---|---|
| Length overall | 29⅜ | 746 | Weight | 2¼ | 63 |
| Length of playing hair | 25¹¹⁄₃₂ | 645 | | | |

# THE PLUCKED INSTRUMENTS

In this category the Hill Collection contains four guitars, all from the seventeenth century and all of high quality, including a rare Stradivari guitar (No. 41), guitars of the most elaborate design, and a special type of guitar called the 'chitarra battente' (No. 39). There are also three citterns: one by Gasparo da Salò from the sixteenth century and two others of seventeenth-century Italian provenance. The last group consists of five English guitars, a species of latter-day citterns, all by English makers between 1750 and 1800.

Of these three species of instruments, the guitar is the only one with a continuous history to the present day. However, the early guitar differed considerably from the type we know now. The guitars in the Hill Collection illustrate this. For instance, compared with the familiar 'figure 8' pattern of the modern guitar, the Stradivari guitar (No. 41) is narrower in the body, and its waist is indented less deeply and more highly placed. The fingerboard-neck is flush with the table and emerges from it. In these early guitars, the head is often quadrangular, and sometimes it is bent back slightly. The pegs are normally set into the head and tuned from the back, but some early guitars had a pegbox, a scroll or carved head, and lateral pegs (see the illustration in Mersenne, *Harmonie Universelle*, 1636). The tuning and stringing were also different (see below). However, like the modern guitar, the early instrument had a rose hole (often elaborate), a bridge glued to the belly, deep ribs, and flat back; and it had metal frets set into the fingerboard.

It is difficult to be precise about the origin of the guitar. Tinctoris speaks of it at the end of the fifteenth century under the Latin name *ghiterra* or *ghiterna*, and he says that it was invented by the Catalans, adding that it was rarely used because of the thinness of sound. There is not much doubt that the guitar originated in Spain. Quite likely it was an off-shoot of the vihuela de mano, an instrument akin to the guitar in construction, but like the lute in tuning and playing technique.

In the sixteenth century the lute and vihuela de mano stood for an aristocratic tradition, musically and socially. The guitar was a more popular instrument, and it is hardly surprising that the guitar enjoyed an increasing vogue in the sixteenth

34

century. Compared with the lute, the guitar was simpler to make, costing half as much. At the same time, its simpler stringing and tuning made it twice as easy to play. The guitar, having developed and prospered in Spain and Italy, came to France and thence to England. When Thomas Whythorne went to London about 1545, he noted that the guitar and cittern 'were then strange to England, and therefore the more desyred and esteemed'.[1] Two years later the inventory of instruments belonging to King Henry VIII, made at the time of his death (381 instruments in all), included twenty-one guitars. Terms for the guitar in France were: *guiterre* or *guiterne*; and in England, *gittern(e)*—not to be confused with *cittern* (see below).

The usual guitar of the sixteenth century was strung with four courses of gut strings. Three, and sometimes four, of these courses were doubly strung, generally tuned in unison, but sometimes in octaves. The courses were tuned to c f a d' (or in this relationship), and the frets numbered seven or eight. The instrument was plucked with the fingers, and the music played from tablature.

By the end of the sixteenth or early seventeenth century, the stringing had increased to five double courses, the fifth course being added below. At the same time the pitch was raised a tone, giving the five-course tuning: A d g b e'. This was doubtless the tuning of our Stradivari guitar.

In the eighteenth century, another lower course was added, tuned to E, the result being the final tuning: E A d g b e'. It was also then that the stringing was simplified by reducing the double courses to single strings. From this instrument the modern guitar developed through the nineteenth and twentieth centuries, especially in Spain, whose national instrument it is. In this connection one may mention the name of Antonio Torres who established the modern design of the guitar in the middle of the nineteenth century. (For chitarra battente, see No. 39.)

Like the guitar, the cittern's origins are hard to trace. It probably derived from the medieval citole. In spite of Dante's reference to the 'cetra'—by which Dante may have meant the cittern—our first real knowledge of the cittern dates from the sixteenth century. Again, the place of origin is not actually known. The three examples in the Hill Collection are all Italian—one from the sixteenth century—but it is interesting that the Italian theorist, Vincenzo Galilei, says that the cittern (*cetera*) 'was used by the English before other nations.'[2] In any case, this instrument seems to have enjoyed a considerable vogue in Europe during the sixteenth and seventeenth centuries. Terms: *cittern* or *cithern*; *cetera* or *cetra* (It.); *cistre* or *sistre* (Fr.); *Cister, Sister,* or *Zitter* (Ger.).

---

[1] See James M. Osborn, ed., *The Autobiography of Thomas Whythorne* (Oxford, 1961), p. 19. Quoted in Daniel Heartz, "An Elizabethan Tutor for the Guitar" in *The Galpin Society Journal* (May, 1963), p. 16.

[2] Vincenzo Galilei, *Dialogo . . . della musica antica, et della moderna* (Florence, 1581), p. 147.

A number of things that have been said about the guitar could be said in principle about the cittern. It was the poor man's lute, being much simpler in construction, much less difficult to maintain, far easier to make, and much less expensive to buy. It was strung with wire strings and would stay in tune much better than the lute. It was easier to play, easy to hold, and could be hung on the wall—indeed, a kind of hook, resembling a nose, can often be seen on the back of the pegbox (cf. Pl. 31c) by which it could be hung up. The bright tone of its wire strings was well suited to popular tunes and to delineate a part in consort playing. It was, in short, an ideal instrument for the enthusiastic amateur; and it was regularly used to pass an idle hour while awaiting one's turn in those barber shops which thoughtfully supplied citterns to divert their customers.

From the front, the body of the cittern somewhat resembles the shape of a pear, but the instrument is much smaller than the lute. A rose hole is usual. The curious 'wings'[1] at the shoulders are thought to be a vestige of the ancient kithara (also called 'cetra' in Italian). The back of the cittern is flat, and the ribs are quite shallow. In profile, the body outline resembles a wedge since the ribs are shallower at the bottom than at the top (Pl. 31c). The fingerboard is not flush with the body but is glued on top of the neck. Brass or metal frets are set into the fingerboard, thirteen or more, each representing a semitone. Anthony Holborne's *Cittharn Schoole* of 1597 has chromatic frets running up to 'q', which, if 'a' denotes open string, means sixteen frets.[2] The neck itself is quite distinctive: the bass side is thinner than the treble side so that the thumb can reach around easily in playing. The wire strings are attached at the lower end of the instrument, and run over a movable bridge. At the other end the strings are regulated by frontal pegs or sometimes by lateral pegs set in a pegbox, the latter arrangement being general later.

In the sixteenth century the stringing usually consisted of four double courses, and there were two principal tunings, the French: a g d' e', and the Italian: b g d' e'. Both these tunings are so-called 're-entrant' tunings with the fourth (lowest placed) course higher than the third, as in the modern ukelele, for simplifying chords. The strings were probably made of overspun brass for the lowest-sounding string (g), steel for the top string, and plain brass for the other two. Later a fifth course was added, and the usual tuning became: d a g d' e'. Of the three citterns in the Hill Collection, only one uses a five-course stringing; one has six courses, and the other seven—a fact that points to later additions or changes.

In the music of the sixteenth and seventeenth centuries, the cittern functioned

[1] These cittern 'wings'—knob-like projections from both shoulders of the instrument—should not be confused with 'wings' on violins or viols (cf. p. 13, note 1, above).
[2] See Thurston Dart, "The Cittern and its English Music" in *The Galpin Society Journal* (March, 1948), p. 52.

primarily as an ensemble (not solo) instrument, just as the modern guitar provides a harmonic background in dance orchestras today. By the end of the seventeenth century the cittern was yielding place to the more fashionable guitar, and the last of the cittern books in England, *Musick's Delight on the Cithren*, published by Playford in 1666, records a doleful lament:

of late years all Solemn and Grave Musick is much laid aside, being esteemed too heavy and dull for the light Heels and Brains of this Nimble and wanton Age: Nor is any Musick rendred acceptable, or esteemed by many, but what is presented by Foreigners; Not a City Dame though a Tap-Wife, but is ambitious to have her Daughters Taught by Mounsieur La Novo Kickshawibus on the Gittar, which Instrument is but a new (old one) used in London in the time of Q. Mary . . . being not much different from the Cithren, only that was strung with Gut-strings, this with Wyre, which was accounted the more sprightly and Cheerful Musick, and was in more esteem (till of late years) than the Gittar. . . .[1]

In spite of Playford's implied prediction of a rosy future for the guitar, it had little success in early eighteenth-century England. This explains how, after the middle of the eighteenth century, a species of cittern came to be called the 'English guitar' and could be reintroduced as a novelty. This instrument, which had a short span of life, is clearly derived from the earlier cittern, but there are various changes. The body is larger than the cittern of the sixteenth–seventeenth century, and the neck is broader and shorter, giving the appearance of a less elegant form. The wire stringing is still carried from the lower end over a bridge to a pegbox with lateral pegs; or to a special machine head (Pls. 34, 37) which permits the strings to be tightened by a watch-key inserted at the top of the head. The fingerboard is glued to the neck but it does not extend over the body. Metal frets are sunk, as usual, into the fingerboard.

A special feature of these instruments is the *capotasto*, literally 'head of the touch', meaning the nut or raised projection at the top of the fingerboard. The term often meant, as it does in the instruments of the Hill Collection, a movable device which can be placed at a point (or points) lower down the fingerboard to raise the pitch of all the strings by a semitone (tone, minor third, and so on). (See Pls. 34–37).

The ribs of the 'English guitars' are deeper than those of the citterns and fairly uniform in depth throughout. The neck is also equally thick on the bass and treble side. The 'wings' at the shoulders of the body have disappeared. A typical stringing is six double courses tuned to c′ e′ g′ c′ ′ e′ ′ g′ ′, but one of the instruments in the Hill Collection has six strings consisting of four double and two single courses, and another instrument has five double courses. The 'English guitars', the last of the citterns, disappeared about 1800.

[1] Quoted in Thurston Dart, op. cit., p. 59.

# CITTERNS

**31** (D. 4:2) CITTERN by Gasparo da Salò, Brescia, *c.* 1560 (?).
Plate 31 (a, b, c, d, e, f)
Label: none visible, but the maker's name is branded on the button of the back
(Pl. 31f)

A wood of lattice appearance (cedar of Lebanon), varnished golden-brown, is used
for the belly (cf. remarks to Nos. 2 and 9). Double purfling emphasizes the outline
of the belly, but there is no purfling on the back. Maple is used for the ribs, head,
neck, and back, the latter being a reddish-brown colour. The body has the typical
wedge profile. The rose hole is gilded, and 'wings' adorn the shoulders. The pegbox,
decorated with the carved head of a female figure wearing a ruff, has a hook at its
back (Pl. 31c, e); and where the pegbox joins the neck, it is cut away to give more
room to the outer strings (cf. Pl. 31d and remarks to No. 4). The fingerboard, frets,
and bridge are not original. The pegs were made by the Hills. There are eleven
strings, grouped as four double courses and three single courses, the latter being at
the left side as one looks directly at the instrument (i.e. the bass side). In its present
form, in short, this instrument is strung, not like a typical four- or five-course
cittern, but rather as an eighteenth century-French cistre, which typically used
eleven strings gathered in seven courses on the fingerboard.

Hill Gift, 1939.
*Annual Report*, 1939, p. 27 (where No. 31 is described as a 'cetra', the Italian equivalent of 'cittern').

| MEASUREMENTS | *Inches* | *Millimetres* |
|---|---|---|
| Length overall | $29\frac{1}{4}$ | 743 |
| Length of body | $13\frac{15}{16}$ | 353 |
| Width | $8\frac{3}{4}$ | 222 |
| Depth of sides | $1\frac{3}{4}$—$\frac{9}{16}$ | 45–15 |
| Length of fingerboard | $12\frac{1}{16}$ | 306 |
| String length | $17\frac{13}{16}$ | 453 |

# 32 (D. 4:4) CITTERN, Italian, seventeenth century.
Plate 32 (a, b, c)
Label: none

This cittern is possibly of Venetian or Neapolitan make. The elaborate open-work of the rose hole suggests Spanish influence. The three-tier rose shows traces of having been gilded. The slightly arched belly is made of coarse pine, varnished a yellow-brown. The purfling is entirely inked on, including the triple purfling of the rose. The edge-bead consists of alternate strips of differently coloured woods. The back, varnished a golden-brown, is made of maple cut on the slab, the centre strip of darker wood, and the sides of wood similar to the back. The neck and head are sycamore. 'Wings' decorate the shoulders. The pegbox terminates in the head of a negro carved in ebony with bulbous white eyes. There is open-work at the back of the pegbox but no hook (cf. No. 31). Nine lateral pegs carry five courses of strings, four of them double (the single course is the one at the extreme left as one looks at the front). There are also seventeen frets spaced in the 'French' fashion: that is, some of the frets are placed a full tone apart to avoid a problem of intonation in untempered tuning (see Thurston Dart, op. cit., p. 48).

Presented in 1948 by Mr. A. Phillips Hill.
*Annual Report*, 1948, p. 45, where No. 32 is described as a cetra.

| MEASUREMENTS | Inches | Millimetres |
|---|---|---|
| Overall length | $29\frac{7}{8}$ | 760 |
| Length of body | $14\frac{1}{2}$ | 369 |
| Width | $9\frac{5}{32}$ | 233 |
| Depth of sides | $1\frac{31}{32}-1\frac{1}{16}$ | 50–27 |
| Length of fingerboard | $12\frac{1}{2}$ | 317 |
| String length | 19 | 483 |

# 33 (D. 4:3) CITTERN, Italian, seventeenth century.
Plate 33 (a, b, c, d, e, f)
Label: none visible.

An instrument of construction and design quite similar to No. 33 is in the Conservatoire National de Musique at Paris, and is attributed (probably erroneously) to Antonio Stradivari. The Paris instrument is illustrated in full colour in Hipkins and Gibb, *Musical Instruments* (London, 1921, first published 1888), where it is labelled 'Cetra by Antonius Stradivarius'—on what authority is not said. Hipkins and Gibb say further that 'it belongs to the violinist Alard' (i.e., in 1888). By way of contrast, the cittern in the Hill Collection was described by the Ashmolean Museum in 1939 (*Annual Report*, pp. 27–28) as a 'cetra, probably Venetian, of about 1600 by an unknown maker'—a description that is probably nearer the truth than the Stradivari attribution.

The cittern in the Hill Collection is elaborately carved and decorated. The back of maple, patterned like a shell, is comprised of six fluted panels meeting at the base of the neck. The varnish is golden-brown. The inlaid double purfling is carried around the inside edge of the outline of both top and back. Similar lines of double purfling carry out a design on the ribs. A rose hole of decorative design is set in the table of pine of irregular grain, varnished a golden-brown. The head and back of the pegbox are most elaborately carved, the head representing a handsome lady the top of whose coiffure is decorated with a small blue stone (Pl. 33d). From the fantastic human forms carved on the back of the pegbox (Pl. 33b) there emerges a hook looking much like a nose (Pl. 33e). Carvings further adorn the 'wings' and the button of the back (Pl. 33f, b), those on the latter representing Adam and Eve in the garden. The bridge is also carved (the ivory top is not original).

Twelve strings, gathered in six double courses, are regulated by frontal pegs. The latter are not original but were made by the Hills. There are traces of eighteen peg holes (original?), now stopped up (cf. Pl. 33d). The fingerboard of nineteen frets, some of which are much repaired, is cut away slightly at its lowest extremity (see also No. 31 in this respect).

Hill Gift, 1939. *Annual Report*, 1939, pp. 27–8.

| MEASUREMENTS | Inches | Millimetres |
|---|---|---|
| Length overall | $31\frac{1}{2}$ | 800 |
| Length of body | $14\frac{9}{16}$ | 370 |
| Width | $9\frac{3}{16}$ | 234 |
| Depth of sides | $1\frac{3}{4}$–$\frac{17}{32}$ | 45–14 |
| Length of fingerboard | $12\frac{3}{16}$ | 310 |
| String length | $18\frac{5}{16}$ | 465 |

# ENGLISH GUITARS

34 (D. 1:1) ENGLISH GUITAR by J. N. Preston, London, working 1734–70 (watch-key tuning).
Plate 34 (a, b, c)

Label: 'Preston Inventor' is engraved on the head; 'Preston Maker London' is stamped on the back of the pegbox.

The table is made of pine, varnished an orange-brown colour, and the back and sides of figured sycamore are similarly varnished. The rose hole is inlaid with alternate strips of ivory and ebony, the same materials being used for the bridge. There are six courses of strings (the upper four of them double) and twelve frets. The capotasto has four positions. The tuning is engraved on the head—C E G C E G —and the strings are tuned by a watch-key inserted in holes at the top of the machine mechanism (=watch-key tuning). To allow easy access of the watch-key, the upper end of the head describes a 'U' in profile. The face of the head is decorated with an inlaid star pattern.

Nos. 34–38 were all presented by Mr. A. Phillips Hill.
*Annual Report*, 1948, p. 45 (described as 'English citterns').

| MEASUREMENTS | *Inches* | *Millimetres* |
|---|---|---|
| Length overall | 26$\frac{11}{16}$ | 678 |
| Length of body | 13$\frac{31}{32}$ | 355 |
| Width | 11$\frac{1}{2}$ | 292 |
| Depth of sides | 2–3$\frac{1}{16}$ | 51–68 |
| Length of fingerboard | 9$\frac{1}{16}$ | 230 |
| String length | 16$\frac{5}{8}$ | 422 |

35 (D. 1:2) ENGLISH GUITAR by J. N. Preston, London, working 1734–70 (tuning pegs).
Plate 35 (a, b, c)
Label: as in No. 34, 'Preston Maker London' is stamped on the back of the pegbox.

An instrument very similar to No. 34, except that the strings are regulated by ten pegs in a pegbox (not a machine head). The star set in the face of the head is similar to that of No. 34. There are six courses of strings (four of them double), twelve frets, and capotasto with four positions. The wood, varnish, rose hole, and ivory-and-ebony bridge are all practically identical with No. 34. The bridge is original and the pegs probably are.

| MEASUREMENTS | *Inches* | *Millimetres* |
|---|---|---|
| Length overall | 28$\frac{31}{32}$ | 736 |
| Length of body | 14 | 356 |
| Width | 11$\frac{1}{2}$ | 292 |
| Depth of sides | 2$\frac{1}{16}$–2$\frac{3}{4}$ | 53–70 |

| MEASUREMENTS | Inches | Millimetres |
|---|---|---|
| Length of fingerboard | $8\frac{15}{16}$ | 227 |
| String length | $16\frac{9}{16}$ | 420 |

## 36 (D. 1:3) ENGLISH GUITAR by Michael Rauche, working about 1758–70, London, 1770.

Plate 36 (a, b)

Label: the maker's name is painted on the button of the back: Rauche London: 1770.

The table, scalloped in outline, is made of pine, and is varnished yellow-brown. The back and sides are bird's-eye maple, and the back of the head is veneered to match. There are inlaid designs around the edges of the sides and the back of the head and down the centre of the back, the edge of the top and back of the body being inlaid with ivory. The fingerboard and the face of the head are covered with tortoise shell and mother-of-pearl. Additional features are a decorated rose hole, bridge of ivory, and capotasto with four positions (observe the corresponding holes in the back of the neck, shown in Pl. 36b).

The six double courses are regulated by twelve lateral tuning pegs (contrary to Dart, this is not a watch-key tuning), The tuning pegs, which are of a metal, open-ring type, operate rachets which tune the metal peg-heads. There are twelve frets on the fingerboard.

| MEASUREMENTS | Inches | Millimetres |
|---|---|---|
| Length overall | $31\frac{3}{32}$ | 790 |
| Length of body | $14\frac{1}{8}$ | 359 |
| Width (upper) | $9\frac{7}{32}$ | 234 |
| Width (lower) | $11\frac{7}{8}$ | 302 |
| Depth of sides | $2\frac{25}{32}$–$2\frac{7}{8}$ | 71–73 |
| Length of fingerboard | $9\frac{15}{16}$ | 253 |
| String length | $19\frac{3}{32}$ | 485 |

## 37 (D. 1:5) ENGLISH GUITAR by Frederick Hintz, London, 1786.

Plate 37 (a, b)

Label: 'F. Hintz' is stamped on the back of the neck and on the top of the back and also worked into the rose hole (see below).

The table is made of pine, varnished a medium brown; the back, sides, neck, and head, of figured sycamore. The purfling is inked on, as are the decorative circles around the rose hole. The latter is brass of ornamental design, consisting of various instruments around a figure in the centre bearing aloft a scroll on which is

'F. Hintz'. The fingerboard and face of the head are made of tortoise shell and mother-of-pearl, and the capotasto has four positions on the fingerboard. There are ten strings gathered in six courses (four of them double), fifteen frets (with two extra ones for the top course), and a watch-key tuning. At the top of the neck is pencilled 'Preston's New Instruments . . . 1786'.

| MEASUREMENTS | Inches | Millimetres |
|---|---|---|
| Length overall | $27\frac{17}{32}$ | 700 |
| Length of body | $13\frac{31}{32}$ | 355 |
| Width | $12\frac{3}{16}$ | 310 |
| Depth of sides | $2\frac{5}{16}$–$3\frac{1}{8}$ | 58–79 |
| Length of fingerboard | $10\frac{11}{16}$ | 272 |
| String length | $16\frac{3}{16}$ | 412 |

## 38 (D. 1:4) ENGLISH GUITAR by Lucas, London, late 18th century.
Plate 38 (a, b)
Label:  Lucas at Ye Golden Guitar, Silver St.
Golden Square

The table of pine is very similar in outline to No. 37. The back and sides are of sycamore. At the top of the back there is an ornamental ivory inset. The varnish is very dark. The ornamental rose-hole of cast brass is gilded and similar to that of No. 37. The fingerboard and face of the head are made of tortoise shell and mother-of-pearl.

The ten strings are gathered in five double courses, regulated by lateral tuning pegs set in a pegbox. There are thirteen frets but there is no capotasto.

| MEASUREMENTS | Inches | Millimetres |
|---|---|---|
| Length overall | $29\frac{5}{16}$ | 745 |
| Length of body | $13\frac{11}{16}$ | 348 |
| Width | $12\frac{9}{32}$ | 312 |
| Depth of sides | $2\frac{3}{16}$–3 | 55–76 |
| Length of fingerboard | $10\frac{1}{16}$ | 256 |
| String length | $16\frac{5}{16}$ | 414 |

# GUITARS

## 39 (D. 5:1) GUITAR (CHITARRA BATTENTE) by Giogio [Giorgio] Sellas, Venice, 1627.
Plate 39 (a, b, c, d, e, f )

Label: inscribed on mother-of-pearl on the front of the head (Pl. 39e):

Giogio Sellas  
alla Stella in  
Venetia  
1627  
Fecit

This instrument is an elaborately ornamented chittara battente, distinguished from the true guitar by the bulging shape and depth of its back. The term means a 'guitar played (struck) with a plectrum'. Quite probably it was descended from the old 'vihuela de penola'.

The table of pine is elaborately inlaid with patterned designs around the edges and around the rose-hole. The latter is recessed, and birds in tiers inhabit its recesses (Pl. 39f). The back is ebony with ivory inlay, highly decorated by floral ornaments and by figures and instruments on the curved sides, carried on to the back of the neck. The fingerboard is covered with designs on mother-of-pearl (Pl. 39d). The ornamental border of the fingerboard continues along the edge of the table. The front of the head has the maker's name as well as figures of human beings and animals (Pl. 39e). Ten strings are gathered in five double courses, the pegs being inserted and tuned from the back of the head. The frets are missing. Provenance: Puttick and Simpson sale, 8 December 1909.

Hill Gift, 1939.                                   *Annual Report*, 1939, p. 28.

| MEASUREMENTS | *Inches* | *Millimetres* |
|---|---|---|
| Length overall | $37\frac{1}{16}$ | 942 |
| Length of body | $17\frac{17}{32}$ | 445 |
| Width, upper bouts | $8\frac{1}{4}$ | 210 |
| Width, centre bouts | $7\frac{9}{16}$ | 192 |
| Width, lower bouts | $10\frac{1}{16}$ | 255 |
| Depth of sides | $2\frac{9}{16}$–$3\frac{9}{16}$–$3\frac{15}{16}$ | 65–90–100 (centre) |
| Length of fingerboard | $12\frac{13}{16}$ | 325 (neck) |
| String length | $26\frac{13}{16}$ | 681 |

# 40 (D. 5:4) GUITAR by René Voboam, French School, 1641.

Plate 40 (a, b, c, d, e)

Label: on the top of the head (Pl. 40e) the name of the maker is scratched in ivory:

René  
Voboam  
1641

For some years this instrument has been attributed to René Toboin but an examination of the inscription will show that the last two letters of the surname are less likely 'in' than 'am'. The initial letter can hardly be a 'T'; and in view of the fact that there was a family named Voboam making lutes in seventeenth-century Paris, the name must be Voboam. (For a guitar by Jean Voboam, Paris, 1692, see *Hinrichsens's Eleventh Music Book* London, 1961, Pl. 45.)

The table is made of natural pine. There is an elaborately gilded and recessed rose-hole, enclosing a six-pointed rose pattern (Pl. 40d). The rose is bordered by a patterned inlay. The ends of the bridge are extended by a decorative design, and the inlaid edge of the outline of the body is carried upward along the edges of the fingerboard. The latter is ornamented with floral patterns. The back and sides are made of strips of tortoise-shell in patterned arrangement, the inset design being made of mother-of-pearl. The back has two ivory buttons, one at the top and one at the bottom, presumably to keep the instrument from being scratched when laid on the table (Pl. 40b). Ten strings are gathered in five double courses. The tuning pegs are inset and tuned from the back of the head, which is thrown slightly backward. The frets are missing.

Hill Gift, 1939.

| MEASUREMENTS | Inches | Millimetres |
|---|---|---|
| Length overall | $36\frac{7}{8}$ | 937 |
| Length of body | $18\frac{3}{16}$ | 462 |
| Width, upper bouts | $8\frac{1}{16}$ | 205 |
| Width, centre bouts | $7\frac{3}{16}$ | 183 |
| Width, lower bouts | $9\frac{11}{16}$ | 246 |
| Depth of sides | $3\frac{1}{16}$–$3\frac{7}{16}$ | 78–88 |
| Length of fingerboard | $12\frac{5}{8}$ | 321 (neck) |
| String length | $27\frac{3}{8}$ | 696 |

# 41 (D. 5:2) GUITAR by Antonio Stradivari, Cremona, 1688 (1680?).
Plate 41 (a, b, c, d)
Label: carved and filled with mastic on the back of the head:

Ant:ᵇ Stradiuarius<br>
Cremonen:ᵇ F. 1688

This guitar has always been dated 1680 in previous accounts. But if one examines the last digit of the date under a magnifying glass, it becomes apparent that the carved figure is waisted on both sides as it would be with an '8' but not with an 'o' (Pl. 41d).

An *avis rara* among instruments, this guitar by Stradivari is plain in design and little decorated but impressive in its clean, beautiful lines. The table is made of medium-grained pine of natural finish. The back, sides, head, and neck are figured maple, varnished golden-brown. The rose-hole has a simple inlaid ornamental border, the same design adorning the top of the bridge. Narrow black-line stripes run down the middle and sides of the back, the stripes then being carried from the middle of the guitar up on both sides of the neck and head; and the outline of the table is bordered in black. Ten strings are gathered in five double courses, regulated by rear pegs (probably original). There are eighteen frets, the last six extending along the belly.

Hill Gift, 1939. *Annual Report*, 9139, p. 28.

| MEASUREMENTS | *Inches* | *Millimetres* |
| --- | --- | --- |
| Length overall | $39\frac{17}{32}$ | 1004 |
| Length of body | $18\frac{1}{2}$ | 470 |
| Width, upper bouts | $8\frac{15}{32}$ | 215 |
| Width, centre bouts | 7 | 178 |
| Depth of sides | $3\frac{3}{4}$–$4\frac{1}{8}$ | 95–105 |
| Length of fingerboard | $14\frac{1}{4}$ | 362 (neck) |
| String length | $29\frac{3}{16}$ | 741 |

42 (D. 5:3) GUITAR by Antonio dos Santos Vieyra, Portuguese, 17th century. Plate 42 (a, b)
Label:

Antonio

dos S<sup>tos</sup> Vieyra

a feze em

LXA

The label means: 'Antonio dos Santos Vieyra made [this guitar] in Lisbon' [no date]. The table is made of fine-medium grained pine but the back and probably the sides are made of rosewood. Elaborate ornamental figures surround the rose-hole, and other decorative patterns flow from the sides of the bridge and adorn the lower part of the table. The outer edge of the table is defined by ivory and ebony insets. The fingerboard is decorated. Three bold and handsome designs, consisting of curved loops of ivory inset, ornament the back (Pl. 42b). There are twelve strings in six double courses. The pegbox is thrown back and has rear pegs made of ivory, the face of each peg being ornamented with three black dots. The back of the neck and the head are inlaid with narrow strips of ivory. The frets, apparently of gut originally, are missing from the fingerboard.

Hill Gift, 1939.

46

| MEASUREMENTS | Inches | Millimetres |
|---|---|---|
| Length overall | $39\frac{7}{16}$ | 976 |
| Length of body | $18\frac{9}{32}$ | 464 |
| Width, upper bouts | $8\frac{31}{32}$ | 228 |
| Width, centre bouts | $7\frac{1}{2}$ | 190 |
| Width, lower bouts | $11\frac{13}{32}$ | 290 |
| Depth of sides | $3\frac{1}{4}$–$3\frac{11}{16}$ | 83–94 |
| Length of fingerboard | $12\frac{7}{8}$ | 327 (neck) |
| String length | $26\frac{13}{16}$ | 681 |

# THE KEYBOARD INSTRUMENTS

There are two keyboard instruments in the Hill Collection: a virginal, which was in the original Hill Gift (1939), and a large harpsichord donated later (1948).

The harpsichord was the principal stringed keyboard instrument used between 1500 and 1775; and although it existed earlier in primitive forms and continued slightly later in complex ones, the chronological limits just mentioned define the period of its real musical influence. *Harpsichord*, *virginal*, and *spinet* are terms for keyboard instruments which all embody the same principle of tone production by 'plucking' but whose shape and/or mechanism differ in certain particulars. The harpsichord, which may vary from small to large, has a shape similar to a grand piano and its strings run at right angles to the keyboard. The virginal is a small, oblong model, while the spinet (which is not represented in the Hill Collection) has, roughly, the shape of a triangle, the longest leg of which represents the keyboard side.

The central feature of all these instruments is the jack which 'plucks' the string. The jack is a thin oblong of wood into whose top is set a plectrum, either a quill or a pointed piece of leather, hard leather being used only in modern times. Depressing a key on the manual of the instrument raises the jack, causing it to pluck (really, to strike) the string as it slides by. The jack, which has a hinged tongue, slides down again after striking without making the string sound. Each of these oblong jacks is held in a jack-slide, and the oblong piece of wood slides down again either because of its own weight or because its lower end is actually weighted. The jack-rail, a broad strip of wood running above the jacks and containing them, also helps to bounce the jacks back when they hit on the felted under-surface of the jackrail.

In harpsichords of any size, there are two or more sets of strings, tuned either at unison pitch (8-foot pitch), an octave above (4-foot pitch), or, less commonly, an octave below (16-foot pitch). The manual or manuals (big harpsichords generally have two manuals) are able to play these different sets of strings singly or all together by devices which push the whole jack-slide over so that the jacks will engage a particular set of strings when the keys of the manual are depressed by the player's fingers. In early harpsichords, this was done by the simple expedient of pulling the jack-slide over by hand. Later it was done by mechanical devices regulated by knobs (pulled by hand) or by pedals pushed by the feet. A harp stop (sometimes called 'buff') is a special device by which one can dampen a whole set of strings, muting the tone and shortening its period of resonance, almost like a pizzicato. A lute stop comprises another row of jacks to pluck one of the unison (8-foot) stops at a point much nearer the manuals, thus providing a different tone colour and drier sound from the same set of strings. Differences of tone colour depend on the number and combination of the stops engaged. With two manuals and four or even five sets of strings, the possible variety of tone colour is naturally far greater than with a single manual and one or two sets of strings. Similarly, volume is essentially dependent on the number of stops engaged since (unlike the piano) no significant change in loud or soft can be produced by different degrees of pressure from the player's fingers.

# 43 (D. 0:2) VIRGINAL by Adam Leversidge, London, 1670.
Plate 43 (a, b, c)
Label on jack rail: Adamus Leversidge Londini Fecit 1670

When fully cased, this instrument appears as an oblong chest hinged along the front and back. The upper part lifts up and the lower part drops down, revealing a painted under-lid and a similar scene on the interior of the lower panel. The stand supporting the box is an integral part of the whole, not merely a stand. The sound-board is elaborately decorated with a rose hole, flowers, and a bird. The entire inside edge of the box surrounding the soundboard is gilded with designs also carried out on the jack-rail. There are similar designs on the panels in front of the keyboards including an octagonal design in the middle. The compass is four and a half octaves from BB—f' ' '. On the manual the 'accidental' keys are black, while the keys that correspond to the white keys of the piano are golden brown. One set of strings (one string to a note), runs diagonally from the farther left corner to the nearer right corner, starting with the largest (lowest-sounding) strings. The tuning pegs are on the right. The jack-rail runs diagonally across the line of the strings, the jacks being grouped in twos down this diagonal line. Jacks are not adjustable for voicing (as on many modern harpsichords), and each jack must be removed and separately trimmed.

Hill Gift, 1939 (Collection Arthur Hill).

| MEASUREMENTS | *Inches* | *Millimetres* |
|---|---|---|
| Length overall | 67 | 1703 |
| Length, front to back | 21½ | 546 |
| Depth of body without lid | 11¾ | 299 |
| Keyboard length (panel to panel) | 32⅛ | 816 |
| Keyboard length (manual only) | 31 (scant) | 788 |

# 44 (D. 0:1) HARPSICHORD by Jacob Kirckman (1710–92), London, 1772.
Plate 44 (a, b, c)

Label:                    on backboard above upper manual:
                    Jacobus Kirckman Londoni Fecit 1772

This is a fine, large, two-manual harpsichord by the famous English maker Jacob Kirkman (or, as spelled on the case, Kirckman). Formerly in the possession of the sculptor John Bacon (1740–99)—and successively of Dr. Slatter, Mr. Carl Engel, and Mrs. P. E. Bowman—it was presented to the Ashmolean Museum in 1948 by Mrs. Bowman. This harpsichord is remarkable for its complex mechanism, including a Venetian Swell and a 'machine' (see below).

The instrument is housed in a handsome case of veneered walnut with brass fittings, the bandings being of boxwood; and it sits upon a removable stand, which was made for it. There are two manuals with black 'accidental' keys and white (ivory) diatonic keys, as on the piano. The music rack is adjustable and folding. The panels facing the manuals are made of satinwood veneer, decorated with floral designs, two birds, and a centre-piece of instruments. On the back of the strip separating the upper and lower manual is a note that the instrument was repaired in 1870 by G. W. Goss.[1]

There are three sets of strings—two at 8-foot pitch and one at 4-foot—and four sets of jacks. Linkage to the two manuals is provided by the left foot pedal and by means of hand-knobs: two at the upper right and three at the upper left of the front panel above the upper manual, and one on the left side panel. The total compass of the keyboards is five octaves from FF—f′′′. The lowest FF-sharp is missing as was customary in the Antwerp tradition. A rose hole is cut in the soundboard.

On the upper manual there is an 8-foot stop and lute stop; on the lower manual, another 8-foot stop, a 4-foot stop, and a harp stop. One of the unison stops can be played on either the upper or lower manual. The so-called 'machine' (a device first

---

[1] The harpsichord has just been restored to playing condition by Robert Goble (1965; see Annual Report, p. 26).

50

introduced about 1765) is operated by the left foot-pedal, which is unlocked by means of the handknob on the left side panel. The mechanism of the machine is enclosed inside a separate case fixed on the left side of the harpsichord. The effect of pressing down the pedal that operates the machine is to engage the lute stop and to disengage the other stops.

The right foot-pedal operates the Venetian Swell (patented by Shudi in 1769). In effect, it raises, in varying degrees, ten hinged slats set in a wooden frame that fits down snugly inside the entire case of the harpsichord. This permits a limited crescendo and diminuendo.

Presented in 1948 by Mrs. P. E. Bowman.          *Annual Report*, 1948, p. 44.

| MEASUREMENTS | *Inches* | *Millimetres* |
|---|---|---|
| Length overall | $92\frac{3}{4}$ | 2537 |
| Width at end | $10\frac{1}{2}$ | 267 |
| Width at keyboard end | $36\frac{3}{4}$ | 934 |
| Depth of body with lid up | $12\frac{1}{2}$ | 317 |
| Keyboard length (panel to panel) | $35\frac{1}{4}$ | 895 |
| Keyboard length (manual only) | 33 | 838 |

# BIBLIOGRAPHY

The following bibliography contains a selected list of works intended to suggest additional sources of information and illustration. For the most part those sources that are mentioned in passing in the body of the Catalogue are not listed again in the bibliography.

The third section of the bibliography lists the catalogues of certain instrumental collections, and for various reasons the number of catalogues included is not large. Of the many public and private collections in existence, relatively few have been catalogued in print, fewer still have been adequately catalogued, and of these only a small number contain information that is of general historical significance, reliable, and up-to-date. The catalogues by Bessaraboff and Kinsky may be cited as examples of this last category, but they are exceptions.

## I INSTRUMENTS IN GENERAL

Anthony Baines, *European and American Musical Instruments*, London, 1966.

Anthony Baines (ed.), *Musical Instruments Through the Ages*, London, 1961.

Alexander Buchner, *Musical Instruments Through the Ages*, London [1956]. Excellent photographs of instruments.

Francis W. Galpin, *Old English Instruments of Music*, London, 1910.

Frank Harrison and Joan Rimmer, *European Musical Instruments*, London, 1964. Includes a number of splendid plates.

Gerald R. Hayes, *Musical Instruments and Their Music 1500–1750*, 2 vols., London, 1928–30.

A. J. Hipkins and William Gibb, *Musical Instruments*, London, 1888 and later issues. Fine colour plates. Text out of date.

Georg Kinsky, *Geschichte der Musik in Bildern*, Leipzig, 1929; English edition, *A History of Music in Pictures*, London, 1930 and 1937; New York, 1951. Many pictures of instruments.

Sibyl Marcuse, *Musical Instruments: A Comprehensive Dictionary*, New York, 1964.

Curt Sachs, *The History of Musical Instruments*, New York, 1940.

Emanuel Winternitz, *Musical Instruments of the Western World*, London, 1966. Beautifully reproduced photographs.

## II PARTICULAR INSTRUMENTS AND FAMILIES OF INSTRUMENTS

Donald H. Boalch, *Makers of the Harpsichord and Clavichord, 1440 to 1840*, London [c. 1956].

Philip J. Bone, *The Guitar and Mandolin*, London, 1914, 2nd ed., 1954.

David D. Boyden, *The History of Violin Playing from its Origins to 1761*, London, 1965.

Thurston Dart, 'The Cittern and its English Music' in *The Galpin Society Journal*, vol. I (1948).

E. N. Doring (ed.), *Violins and Violinists*, Chicago, April 1938–December 1960.

Fridolin Hamma, *Meisterwerke Italienischer Geigenbaukunst*, Stuttgart [1931].

Fridolin Hamma, *Meister Deutscher Geigenbaukunst*, Stuttgart, 1948; English translation, London, 1961.

Walter Hamma, *Meister Italienischer Geigenbaukunst*, Stuttgart, 1964.

Alexander Hajdecki, *Die Italienische Lira da Braccio*, Mostar, 1892.

Daniel Heartz, 'An Elizabethan Tutor for the Guitar' in *The Galpin Society Journal*, vol. XVI (1963).

Edward Heron-Allen, *Violin-Making as It Was and Is*, London, 1884.

W. E. Hill & Sons, *The Salabue* [Messie] *Stradivari*, London, 1891.

W. H., A. F., and A. E. Hill, *Antonio Stradivari, His Life and Works (1644–1737)*, London, 1902.

W. H., A. F., and A. E. Hill, *The Violin Makers of the Guarneri Family (1626–1762)*, London, 1931.

Frank Hubbard, *Three Centuries of Harpsichord Making*, Cambridge, Mass., 1965.

Franz Jahnel, *Die Gitarre und ihr Bau*, Frankfurt am Main, 1963.

W. L. Lütgendorff, *Die Geigen- und Lautenmacher*, 2 vols., 4th ed., Frankfurt am Main, 1922.

Max Möller, *The Violin Makers of the Low Countries*, Amsterdam, 1955.

A. M. Mucchi, *Gasparo da Salò*, Milan, 1940.

William C. Retford, *Bows and Bow Makers*, London, 1964.

Joseph Roda, *Bows for Musical Instruments of the Violin Family*, Chicago, 1959.

Raymond Russell, *The Harpsichord and Clavichord*, London, 1959.

Henry Saint George, *The Bow*, London, 1896; 3rd ed., 1922.

Walter Senn, *Jacob Stainer der Geigenmacher zu Absam*, Innsbruck, 1951.

A. P. Sharpe, *The Story of the Spanish Guitar*, London, 1954.

*The Strad*, London, May 1890–.

E. van der Straeten, *The History of the Violin*, 2 vols., London, 1933.

Terence Usher, 'The Spanish Guitar in the Nineteenth and Twentieth Centuries' in *The Galpin Society Journal*, vol. IX (1956).

René Vannes, *Dictionnaire Universel des Luthiers*, vol. I (2nd ed.), Brussels, 1951; vol. 2, 1959.

Louis-Antoine Vidal, *Les Instruments à Archet*, 3 vols., Paris, 1876–8.

Emanuel Winternitz, 'Lira da Braccio' in *Die Musik in Geschichte und Gegenwart*, vol. 8, Cassel, 1960.

Josef Zuth, *Handbuch der Laute und Gitarre*, Vienna, 1926.

## III SELECTED CATALOGUES OF INSTRUMENTAL COLLECTIONS

Nicholas Bessaraboff, *Ancient European Musical Instruments*, 'An Organological Study of the Musical Instruments in the Leslie Lindsey Mason Collection at the Museum of Fine Arts, Boston,' Cambridge, Mass., 1941.

Gustave Chouquet, *Le Musée du Conservatoire National de Musique. Catalogue Raisonné* Paris, 1875; and three supplements by Léon Pillaut.

Carl Engel, *A Descriptive Catalogue of the Musical Instruments in the South Kensington Museum*, London, 2nd ed., 1874.

N. & F. Gallini, *Museo degli Strumenti Musicali* [Comune di Milano], Milan, 1963.

A. Hammerich, *Das Musikhistorische Museum zu Kopenhagen*, Copenhagen, 1911.

Ulrico Hoepli (ed.), *Gli Strumenti Musicali nel Museo del Conservatorio di Milano*, Milan [n.d.].

Georg Kinsky, *Musikhistorisches Museum von Wilhelm Heyer in Cöln*, 4 vols. [vol. 3 was not published], Leipzig, 1910–16. The collection is now in the Karl-Marx-Universitat, Leipzig.

A. W. Ligtvoet & W. Lievense, *Europese Musikeinstrumenten in het Haags Gemeentemuseum*, The Hague, 1965.

Victor-Charles Mahillon, *Catalogue Descriptif & Analytique du Musée Instrumental du Conservatoire Royal de Musique de Bruxelles*, 5 vols., Ghent, 1893–1922.

William D. Orcutt, *The Stradivari Memorial at Washington* [The Gertrude Clarke Whittall set of Stradivari instruments donated to the Library of Congress], Washington, 1938.

Julius Schlosser, *Kunsthistorisches Museum in Wien, Die Sammlung alter Musikinstrumente*, Vienna, 1920.

William Skinner, *The Belle Skinner Collection of old Musical Instruments, Holyoke Massachusetts* (compiled by F. R. Hammond and M. J. Ericsson), Philadelphia, 1933. The Collection is now at Yale University, New Haven, Conn.

Albert A. Stanley, *Catalogue of the Stearns Collection of Musical Instruments* [at the University of Michigan], 2nd ed., Ann Arbor, 1921.

*Carl Claudius' Samling af gamle Musikinstrumenter*, Copenhagen, 1931.

*Catalogue of Musical Instruments at the Victoria and Albert Museum*, vol. 1, Raymond Russell, 'Keyboard Instruments', vol. 2, Anthony Baines, 'Non-Keyboard Instruments', London, 1968

*Catalogue of the Crosby Brown Collection of Musical Instruments of All Nations*, New York, Metropolitan Museum of Art, 6 vols., 1903–14.

*The Erich Lachmann Collection of Historical Stringed Musical Instruments*, Los Angeles, 1950. Excellent photographs by Irvin Kershner. A collection now at the University of California, Los Angeles.

*Printed Photolitho*
*by Ebenezer Baylis and Son Ltd*
*The Trinity Press, Worcester, and London*

*The Hill Collection*

ILLUSTRATIONS

# VIOLS

1

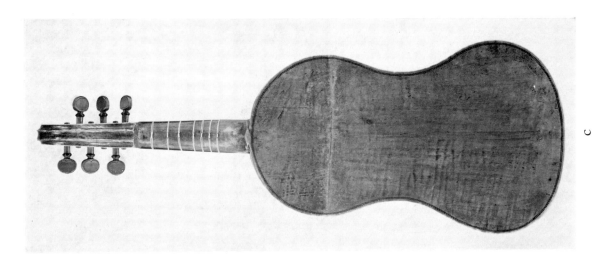

c

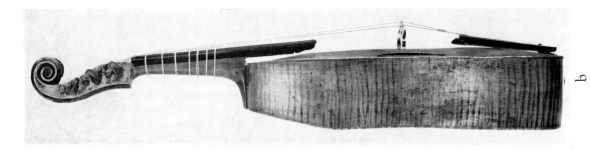

b

a

Treble Viol by Giovanni Maria of Brescia, made in Venice probably between 1500 and 1525

a       b       c

Bass Viol made by Gasparo da Salò, Brescia, late sixteenth century

a                                                    b

Bass Viol, Venetian (maker unknown), sixteenth century

c

d

e

f

a                                                                b

Bass Viol, attributed to John Rose of Bridewell, London, *c.* 1600

c

d

e

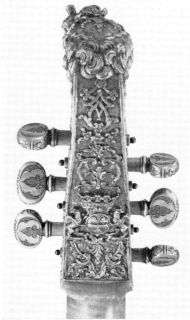

f

a              b

Small Bass (Lyra) Viol by John Rose, London, 1598

c

d

e

f

a                                                  b

Small Bass (Lyra) Viol by Richard Blunt, London, 1605

c

d

e

f

a

b

c

Bass Viol with certain features of a Cello by Antonius and Hieronymus Amati (the 'brothers Amati'), Cremona, 1611

# VIOLINS

a               b

Lira da Braccio by Giovanni Maria of Brescia, made in Venice, *c.* 1525

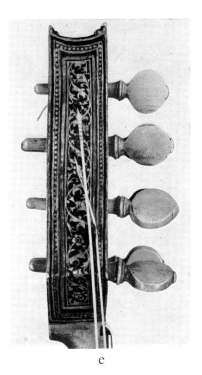

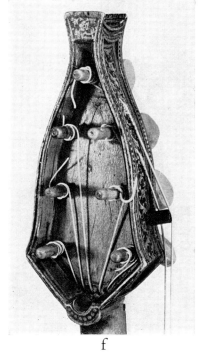

c

d

e

f

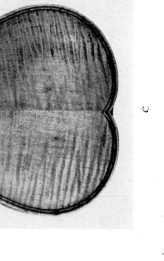

c

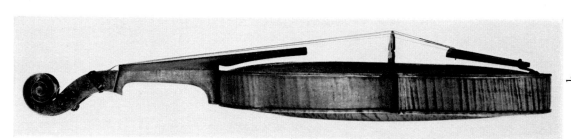

b

a

Lira-Viola by Gasparo da Salò, Brescia, 1561

10

Violin ('Charles IX') by Andrea Amati, Cremona, 1564

a    b    c

Viola ('Charles IX') by Andrea Amati, Cremona, 1574

12

c

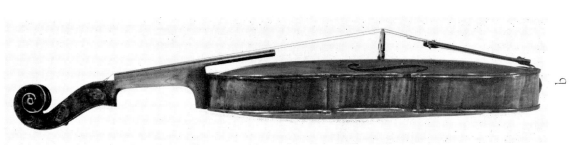

b

a

Viola by Gasparo (Bertolotti) da Salò (1540–1609), Brescia, late sixteenth century

13

Viola by Antonius and Hieronymus Amati, Cremona, 1592

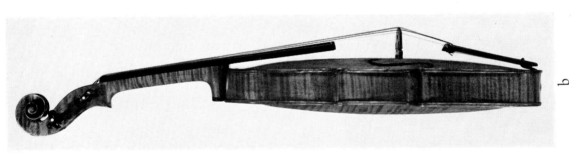

## 14

Violin by Antonius and Hieronymus Amati, Cremona, 1618

c

b

a

15

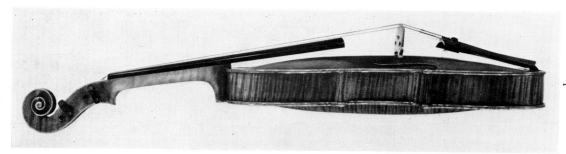

Violin ('Alard') by Nicola Amati (1596–1684), Cremona, 1649

Violin by Jacob Stainer, Absam in Tyrol, 1672

17

c

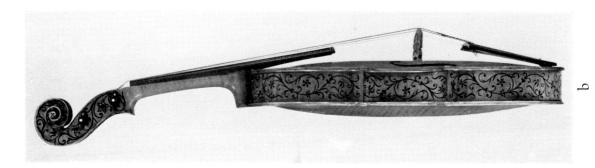

b

a

Violin (inlaid) by Antonio Stradivari (1644?–1737), Cremona, 1683

18

a
b

Violin ('Le Messie') by Antonio Stradivari, Cremona, 1716

c

d

e

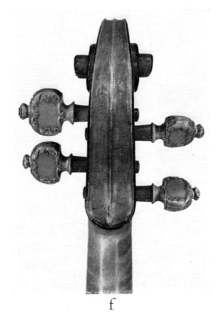

f

# BOWS

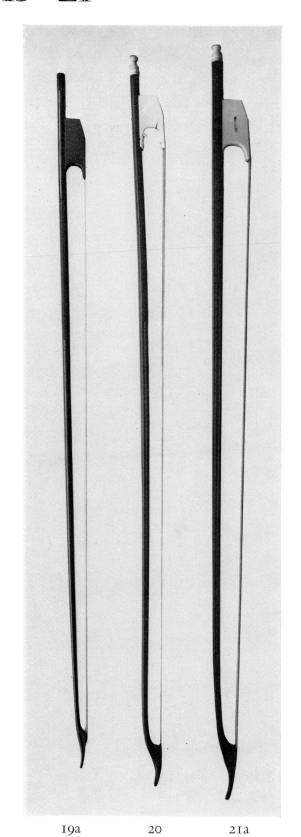

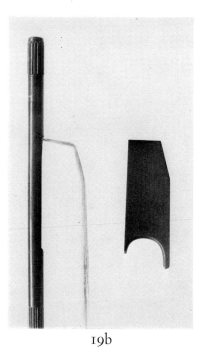

19b

21b

19a, b Violin Bow, slot-notch (or clip-in) type, *c.* 1700

20 Bass-Viol Bow, *c.* 1740–50

21a, b Bass-Viol Bow by Peter Walmsley (or Wamsley), working 1720–44

19a          20          21a

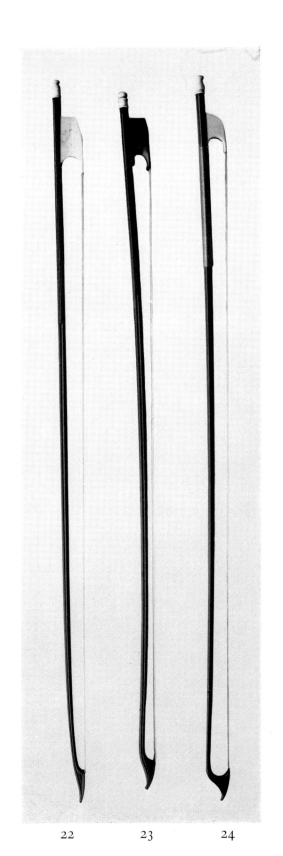

22    23    24

22   Viola Bow by Thomas Smith (working
     *c.* 1756), pupil of Walmsley

23   Violin Bow, *c.* 1740

24   Violin Bow, *c.* 1750

# 25–27

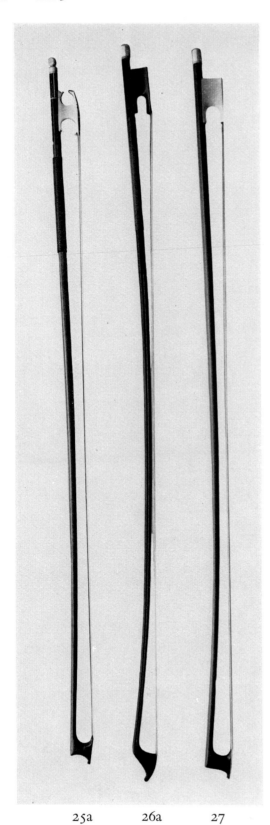

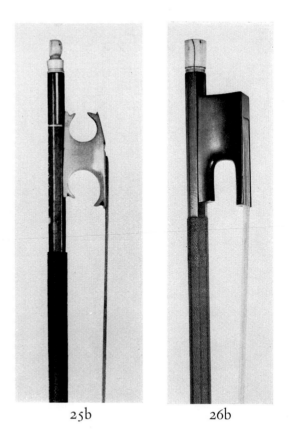

25b        26b

25a        26a        27

25a, b  Violin Bow, c. 1750

26a, b  Violin Bow by Tourte père (father
of François Tourte), c. 1760

27  Violin Bow by Edward Dodd (c. 1705–
1810)

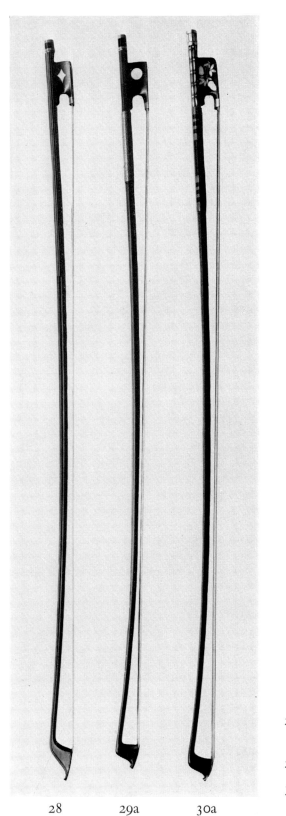

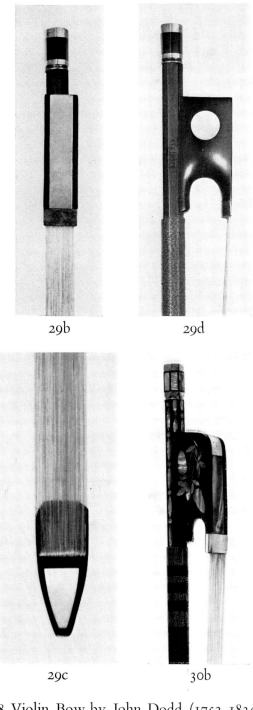

29b

29d

29c

30b

28 Violin Bow by John Dodd (1752–1835), *c.* 1780

29a, b, c, d Violin Bow by John Dodd, *c.* 1800

30a, b Violin Bow, *c.* 1820

28          29a          30a

# CITTERNS

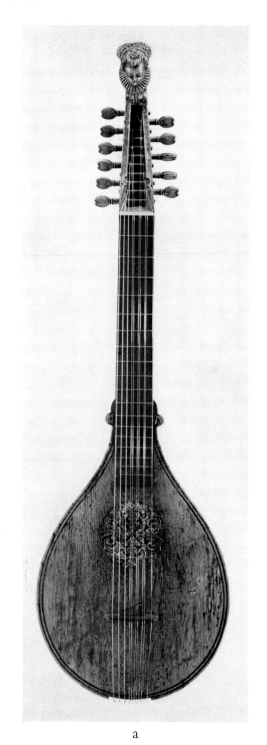

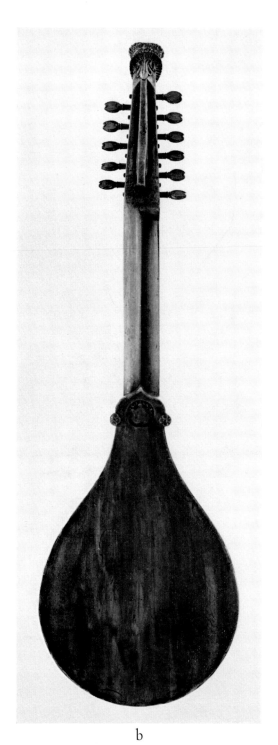

a                                                    b

Cittern by Gasparo da Salò, Brescia, *c.* 1560 (?)

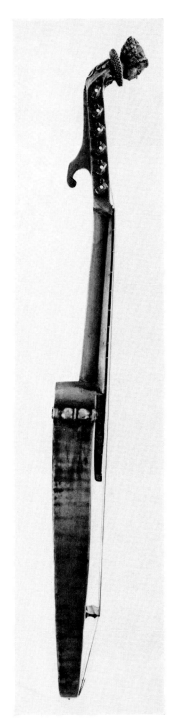

c

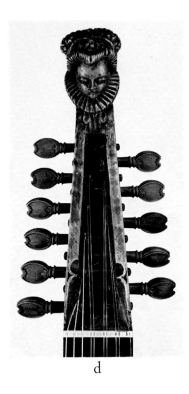

d

e

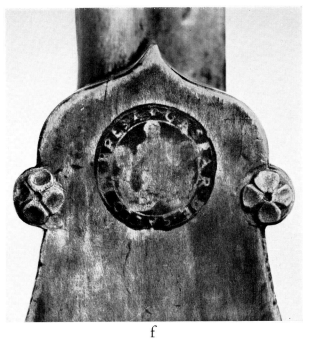

f

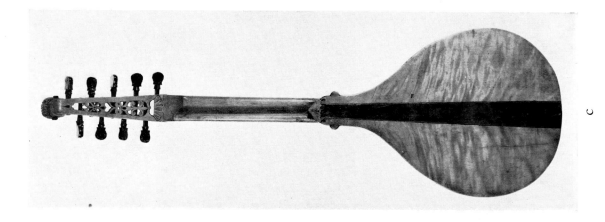

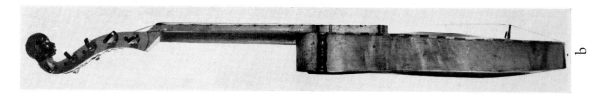

## 32

Citern, Italian, seventeenth century

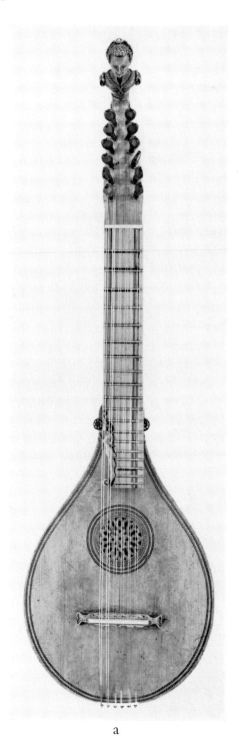

a

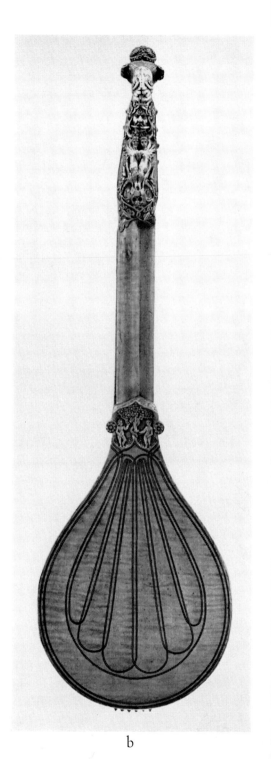

b

Cittern, Italian, seventeenth century

c

d

e

f

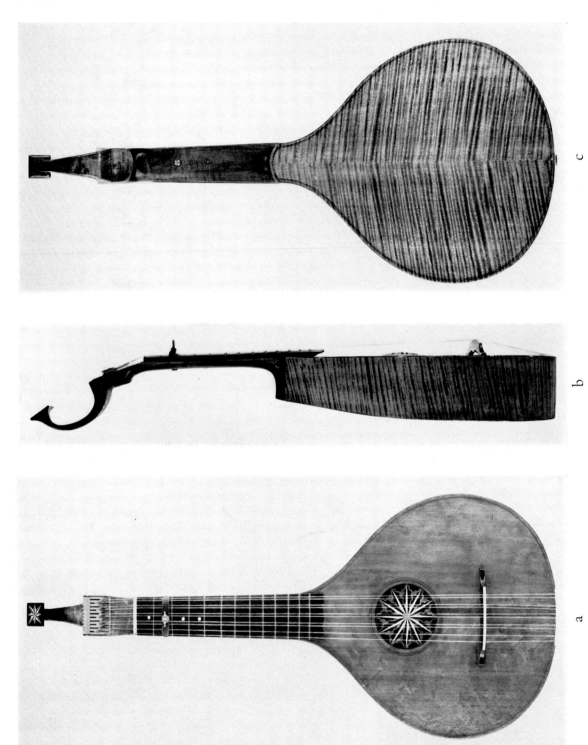

c

b

a

English Guitar by J. N. Preston, London, working 1734–70 (watch-key tuning)

35

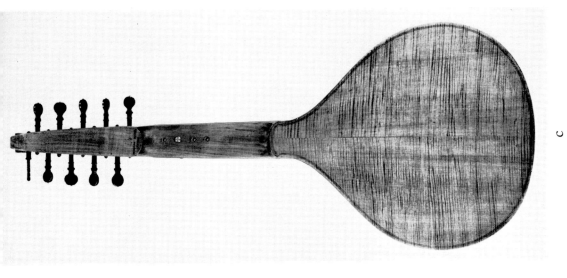

c

b

a

English Guitar by J. N. Preston, London, working 1734–70 (tuning pegs)

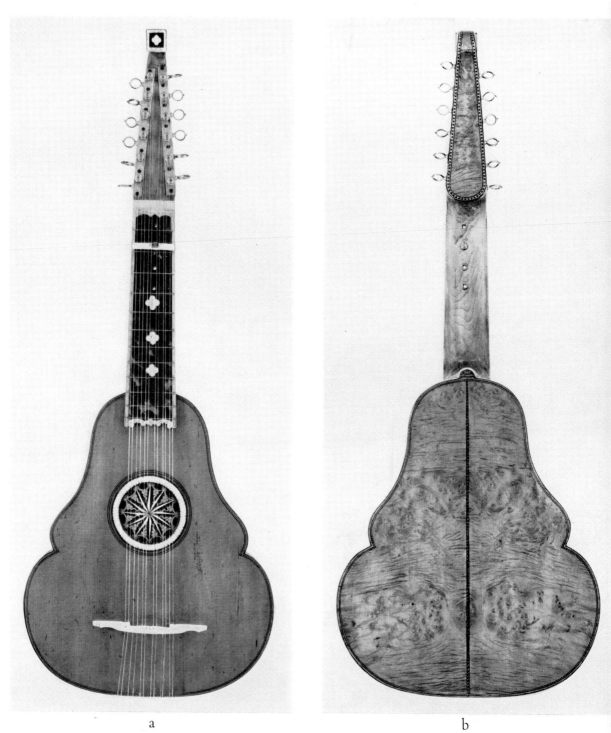

a            b

English Guitar by Michael Rauche, working about 1758–70, London, 1770

a b

English Guitar by Frederick Hintz, London, 1786

a                b

English Guitar by Lucas, London, late eighteenth century

# GUITARS

a                                    b

Guitar (Chitarra Battente) by Giogio (Giorgio) Sellas, Venice, 1627

c

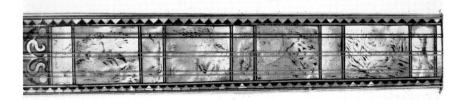

d

e

f

a  b

Guitar by René Voboam, French School, 1641

c

d

e

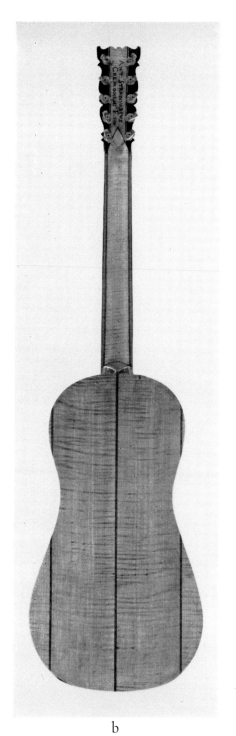

a　　　　　　　　　　　　b

Guitar by Antonio Stradivari, Cremona, 1688 (1680?)

c

d

a                                                                              b

Guitar by Antonio dos Santos Vieyra, Portuguese, seventeenth century

# KEYBOARD INSTRUMENTS

a

Virginal by Adam Leversidge, London, 1670

b

c

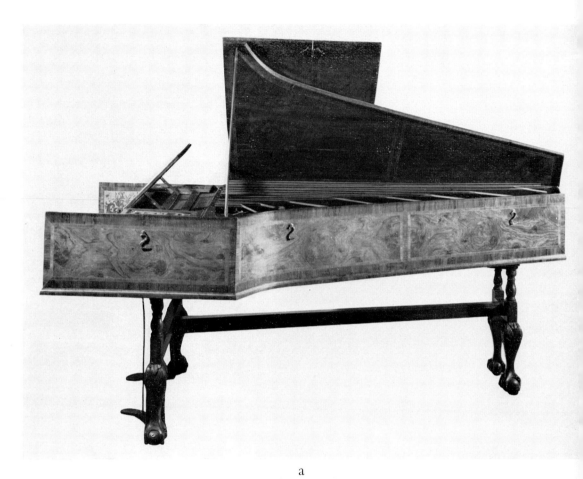

a

Harpsichord by Jacob Kirckman (1710–92), London, 1772

b

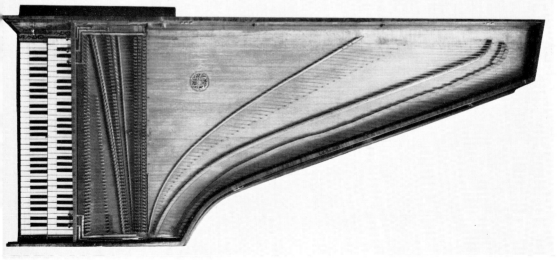

c

*Printed by Ebenezer Baylis and Son Ltd*
*The Trinity Press, Worcester, and London*